ALEBRIJES

Mexican Folk art Colouring book 2

More Fantastic & strange Creatures

Illustrated by
Jorge Lulić

Published by Jorge Lulić Fine Art and Print Publications Alicante, Spain.
The book author retains sole copyright to the design and artwork in this book.
jorgelulic556@gmail.com
www.jorgelulic.com

Welcome to the magical world of Alebrijes

Alebrijes are fun, and in this **Alebrijes colouring book 2** of the series there are 40 exciting original alebrijes illustrations for you to colour at your leisure.

Alebrijes are elusive, whimsical rare and unique creatures.

Some alebrijes have wings, fins, horns, a cat's face, chicken feet, huge teeth, or a bit of everything at once!

Alebrijes have many different patterns, such as stripes, spots, geometrical shapes, flowers, and dots of vibrant colours. Their expressions range from peaceful and playful to cheerful and some even look angry!

Some pages have space left for you to experiment, by drawing your own backgrounds to complement your alebrije picture, which you can fill with your own exiting patterns and textures or you can use the patterns included in this book.

Colouring tips:

- When it comes to colouring, think about using all of the space you have to fill with whichever colours you like the most.

- Original alebrijes are alive with bright and contrasting tones, so keep this in mind when you choose your colours.

- Use either pencils or markers and always test your markers or pencils before your start colouring.

- Remember the ink from markers might bleed through the page, or the inks might run, so slip another piece of paper behind the page you're colouring to protect the page behind.

- Pencils will allow you to blend colours and are very good for fine details. If you like using pencils, buy the biggest selection of colours you can, and keep them well sharpened.

- Lastly: Study the picture carefully before you start, slow down, take your time, and enjoy the process of colouring, and watch your alebrijes come to life!

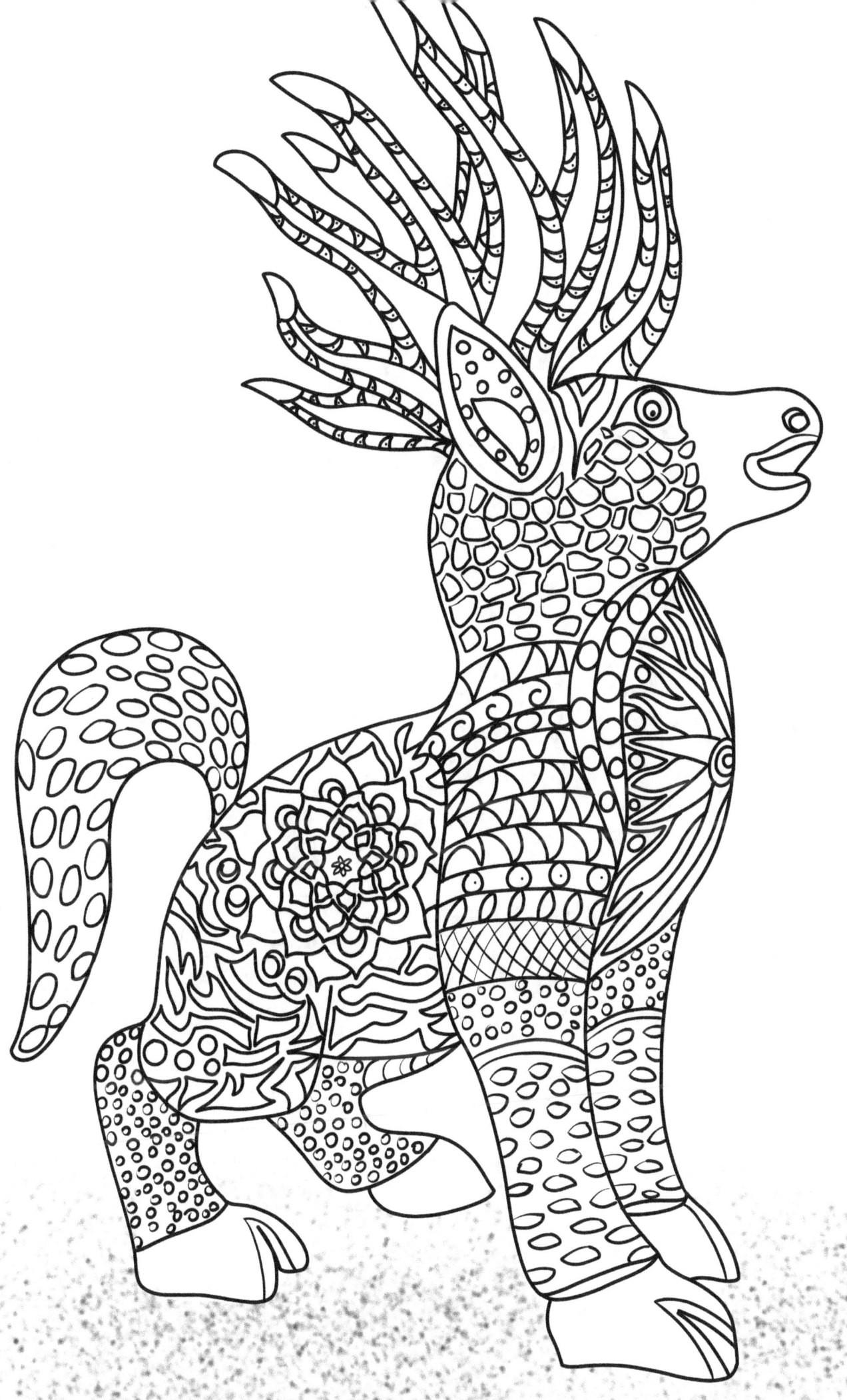

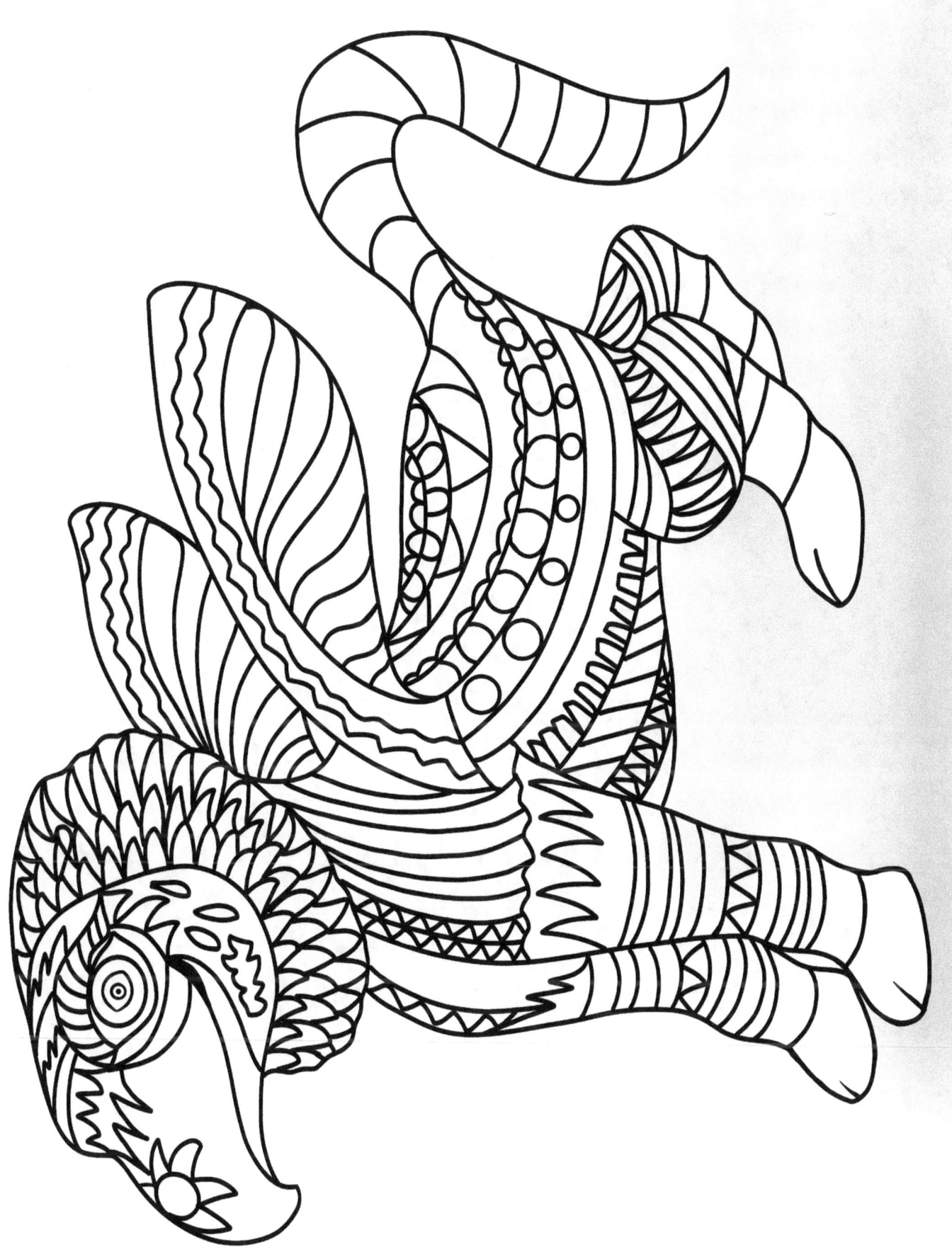

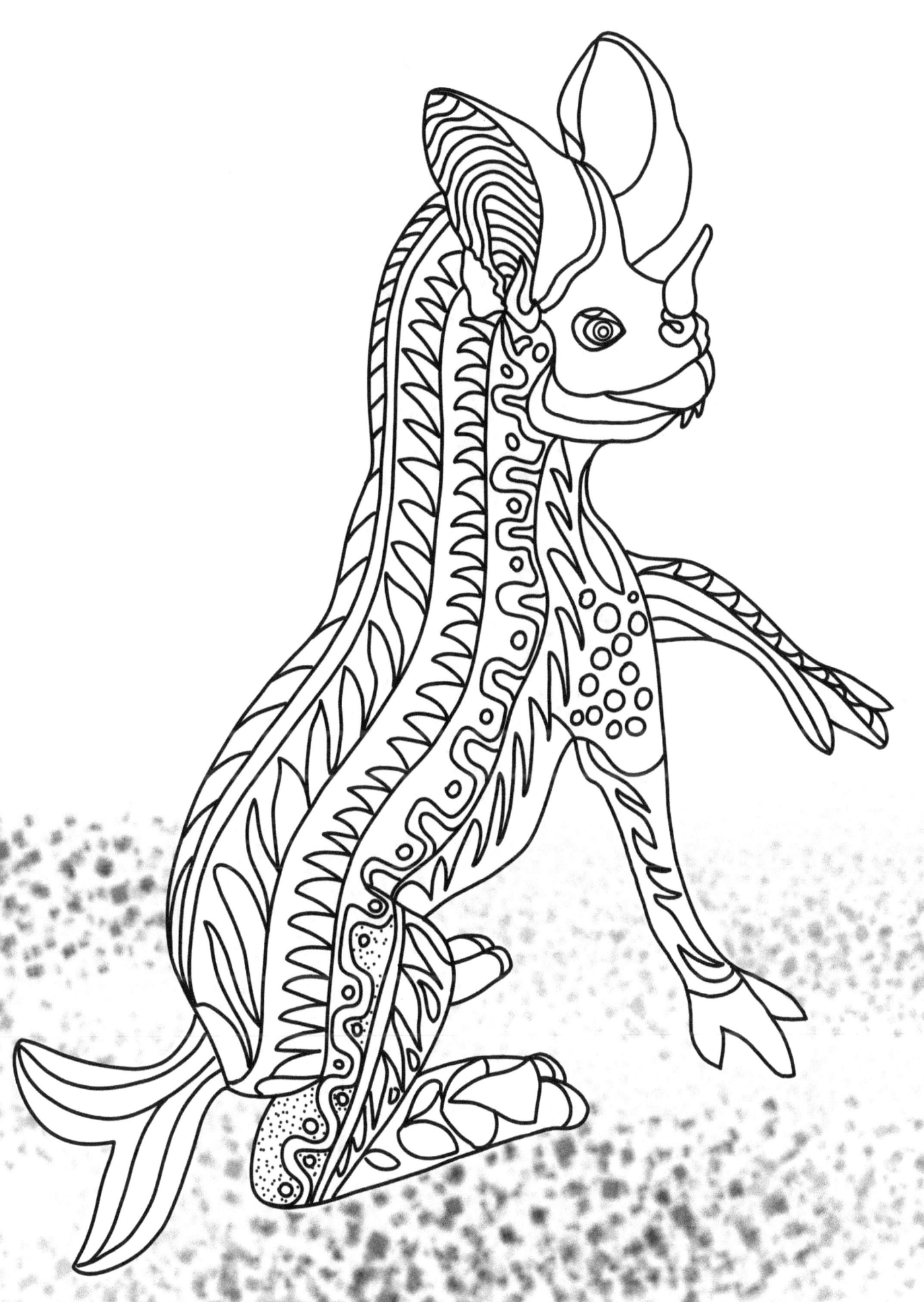

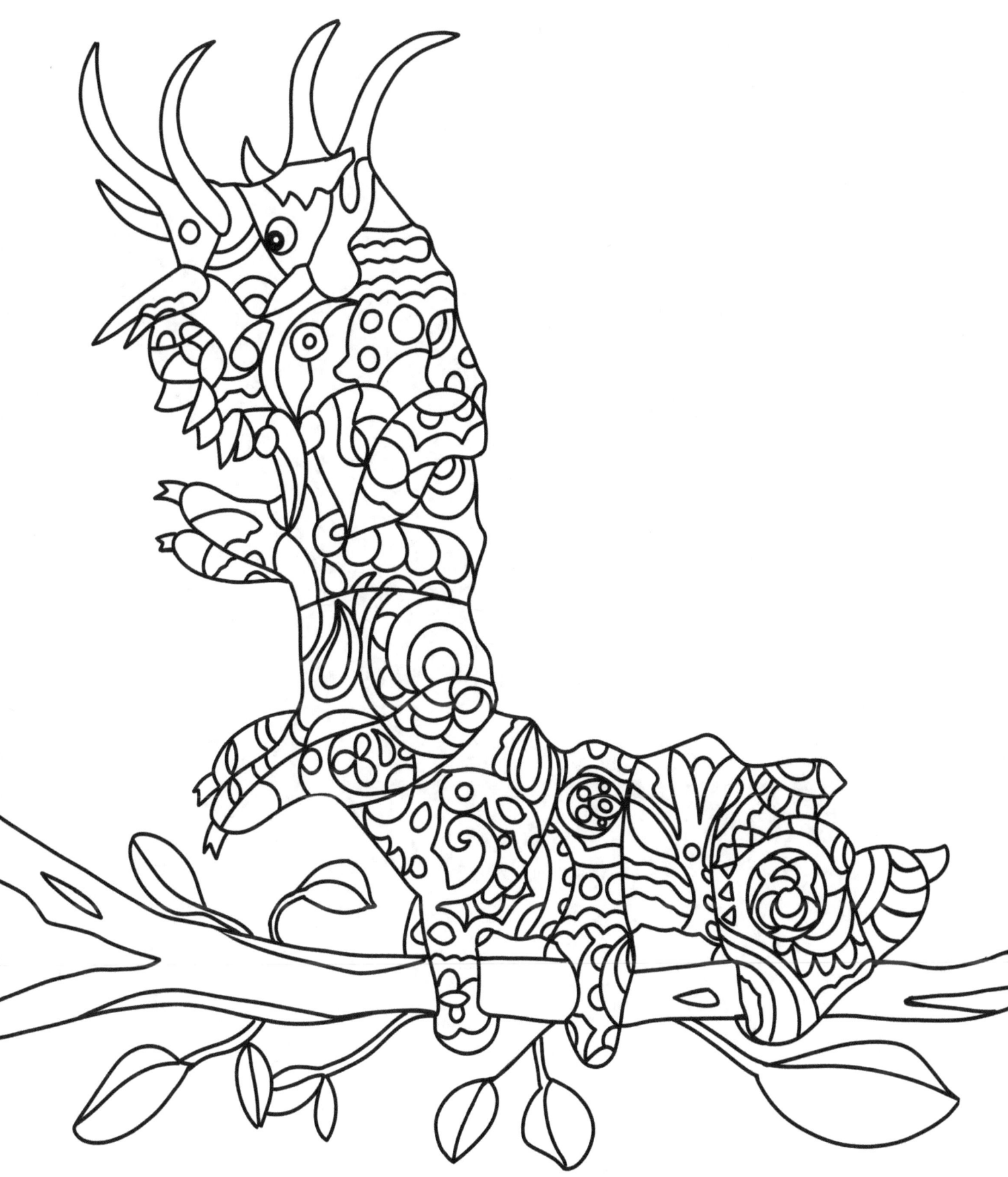

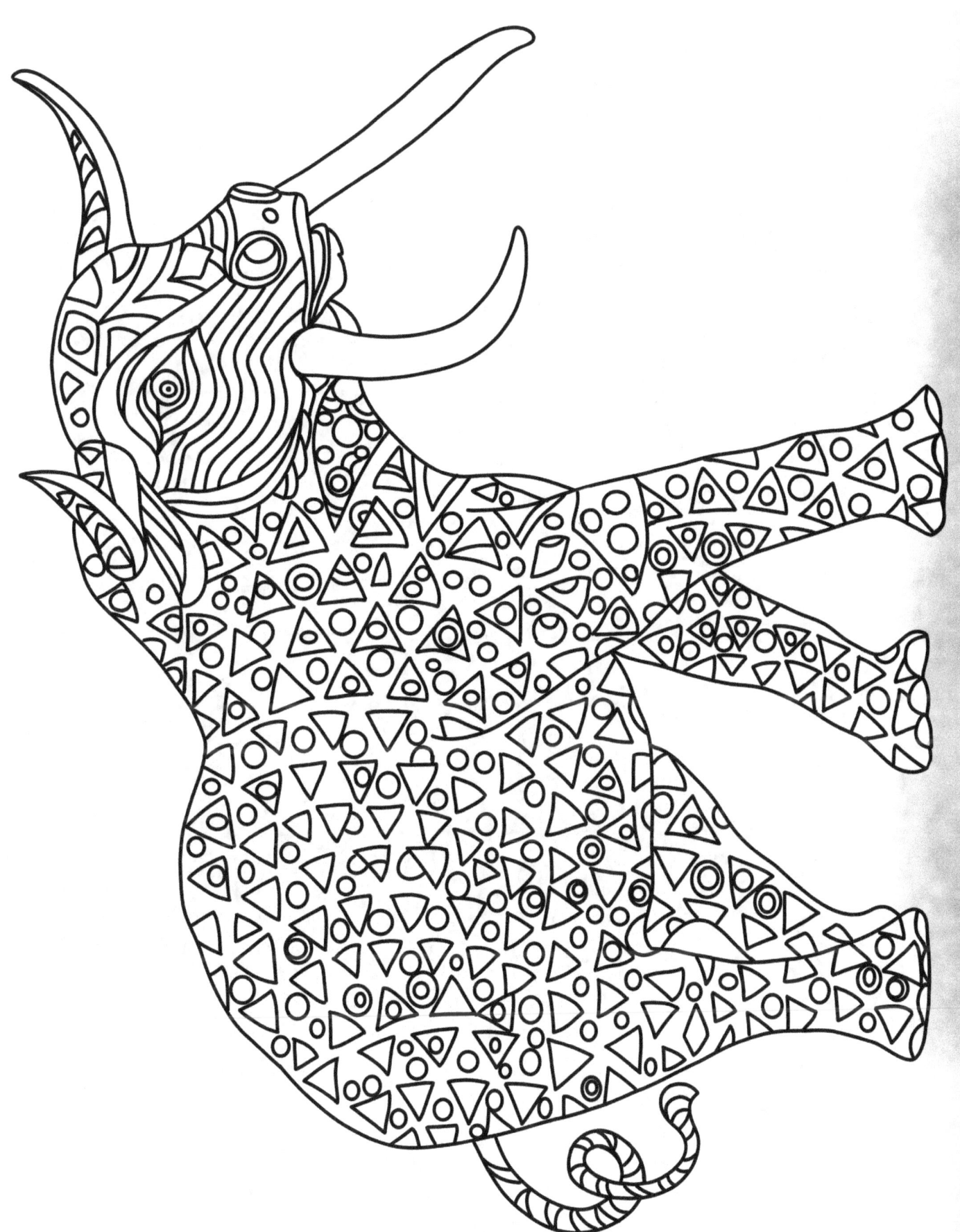

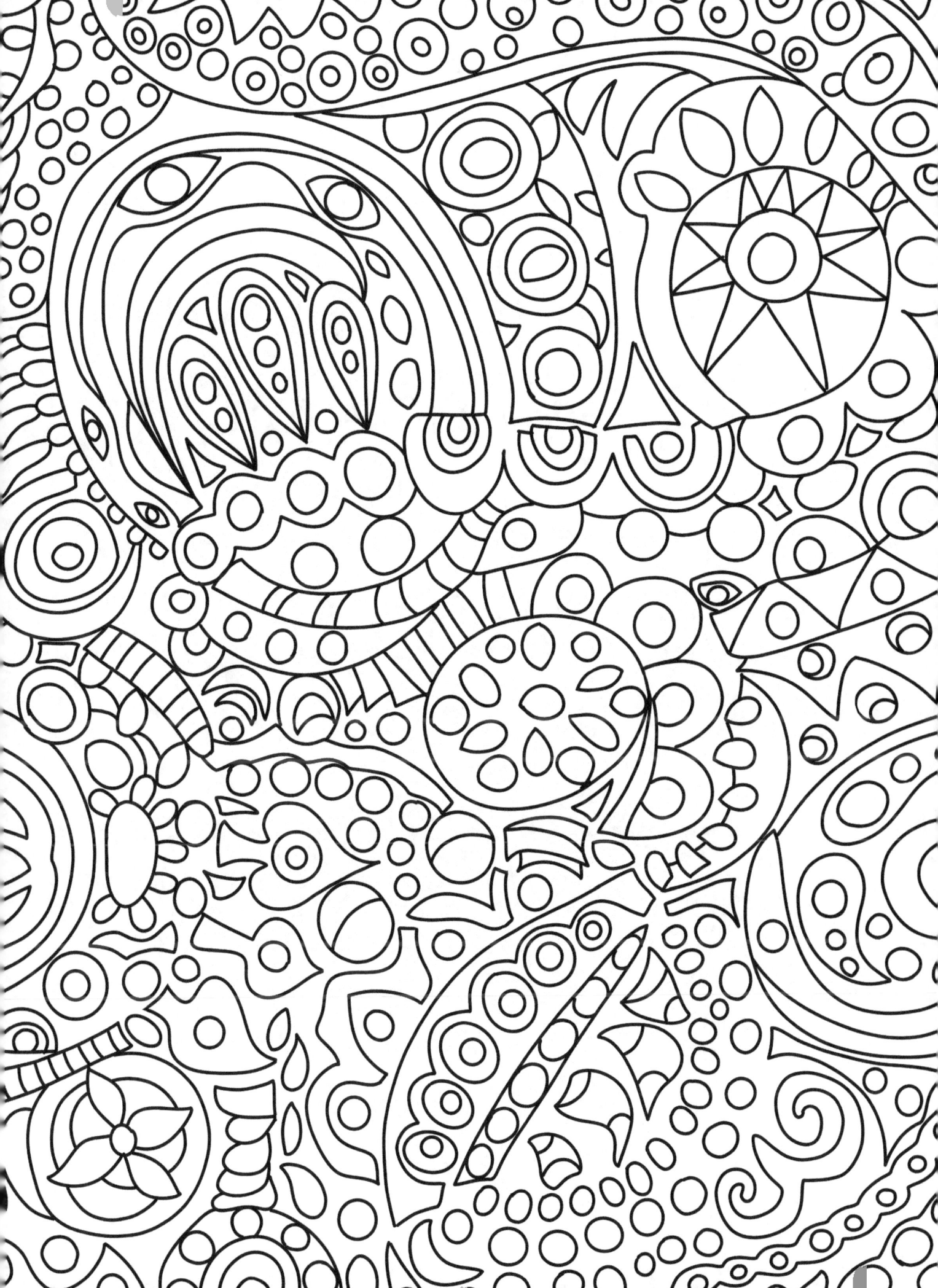

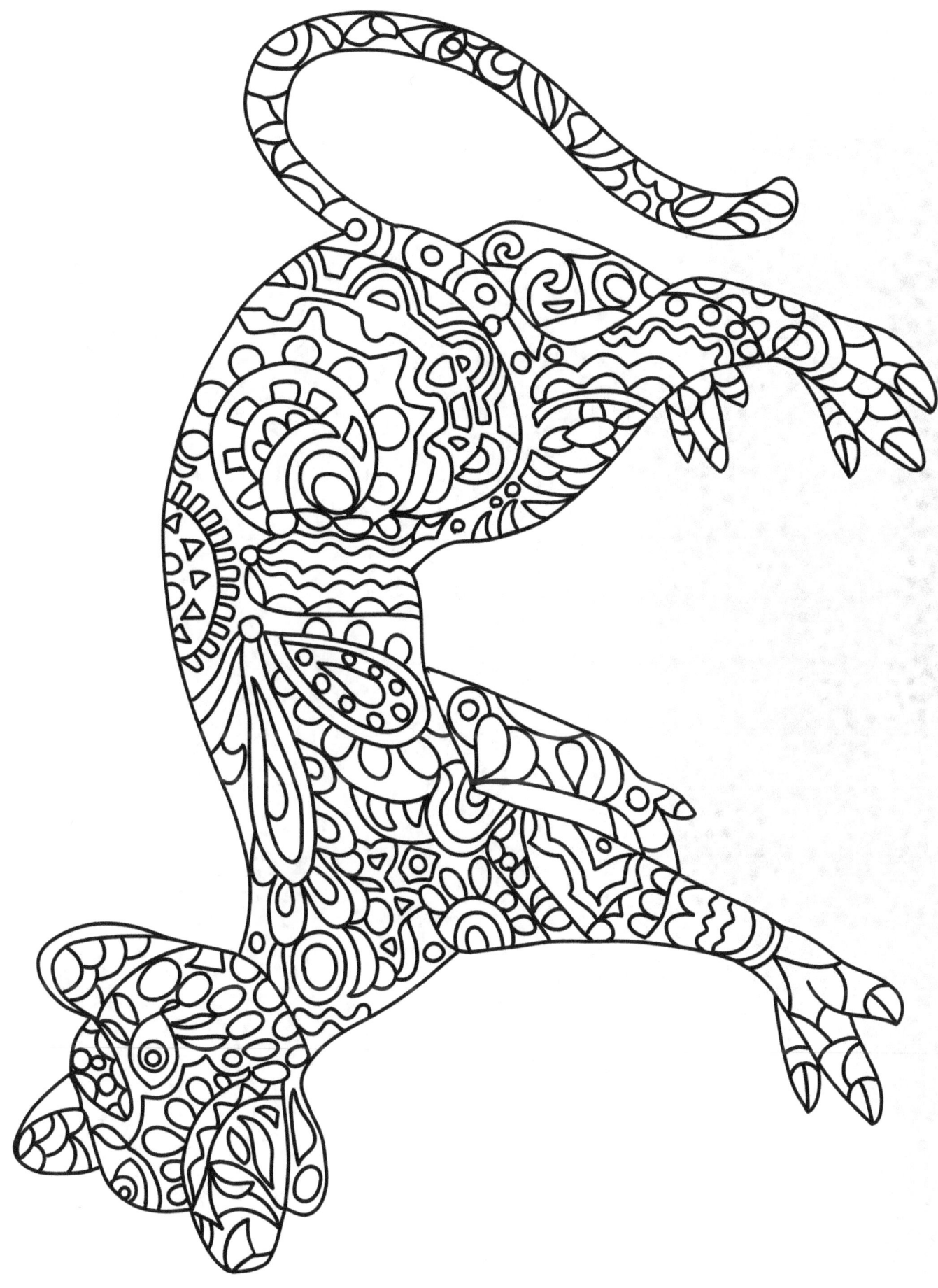

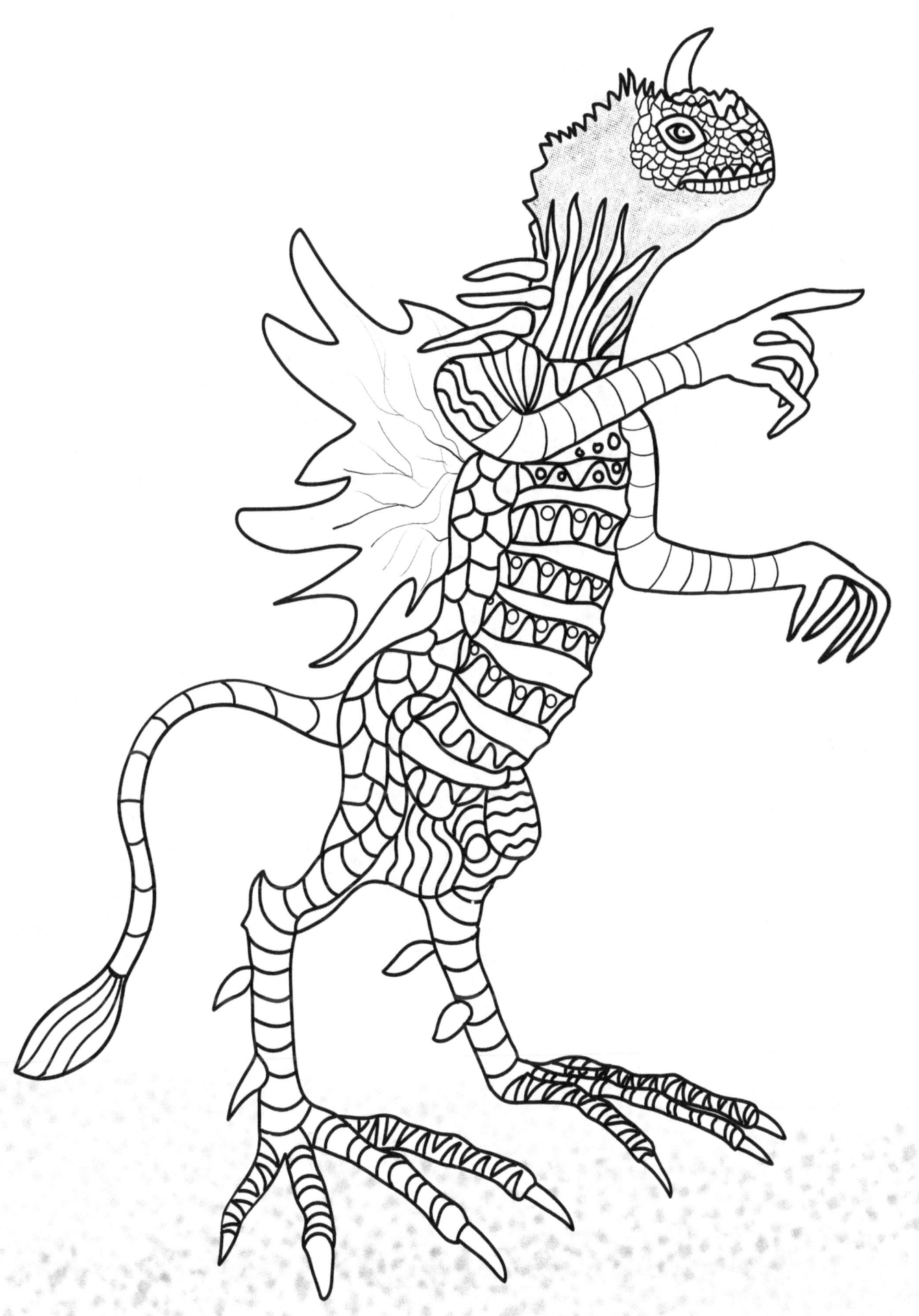

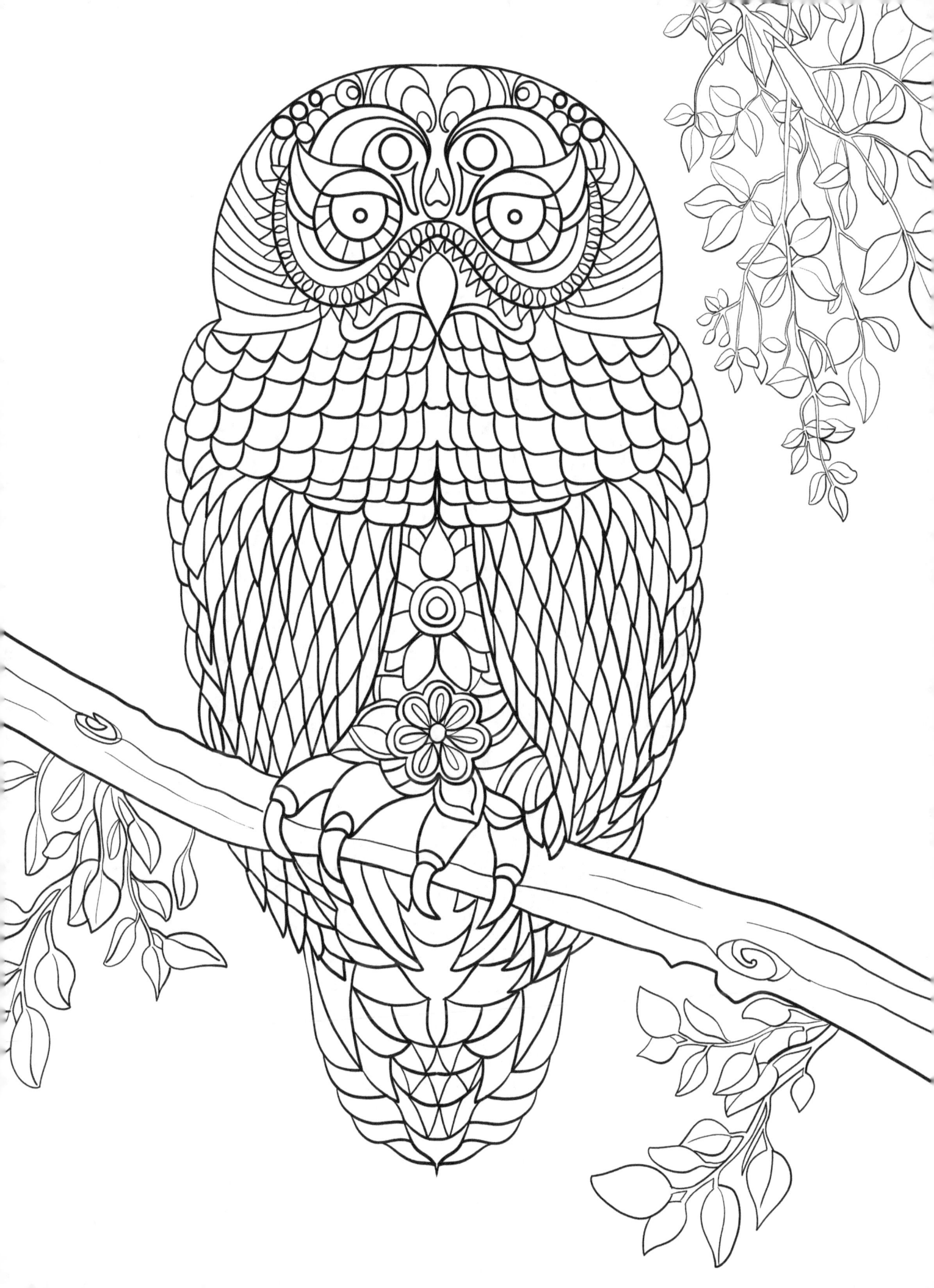

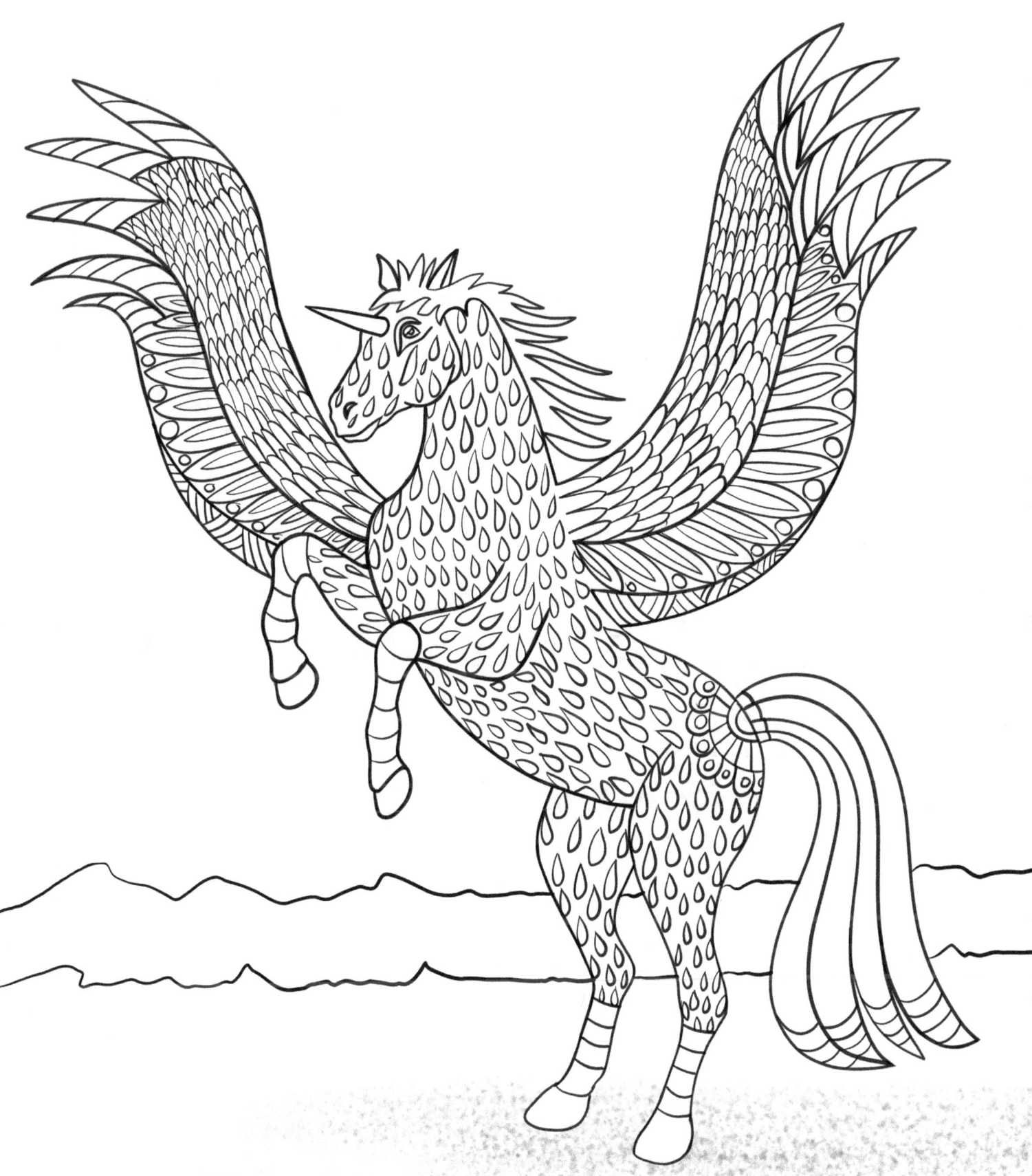

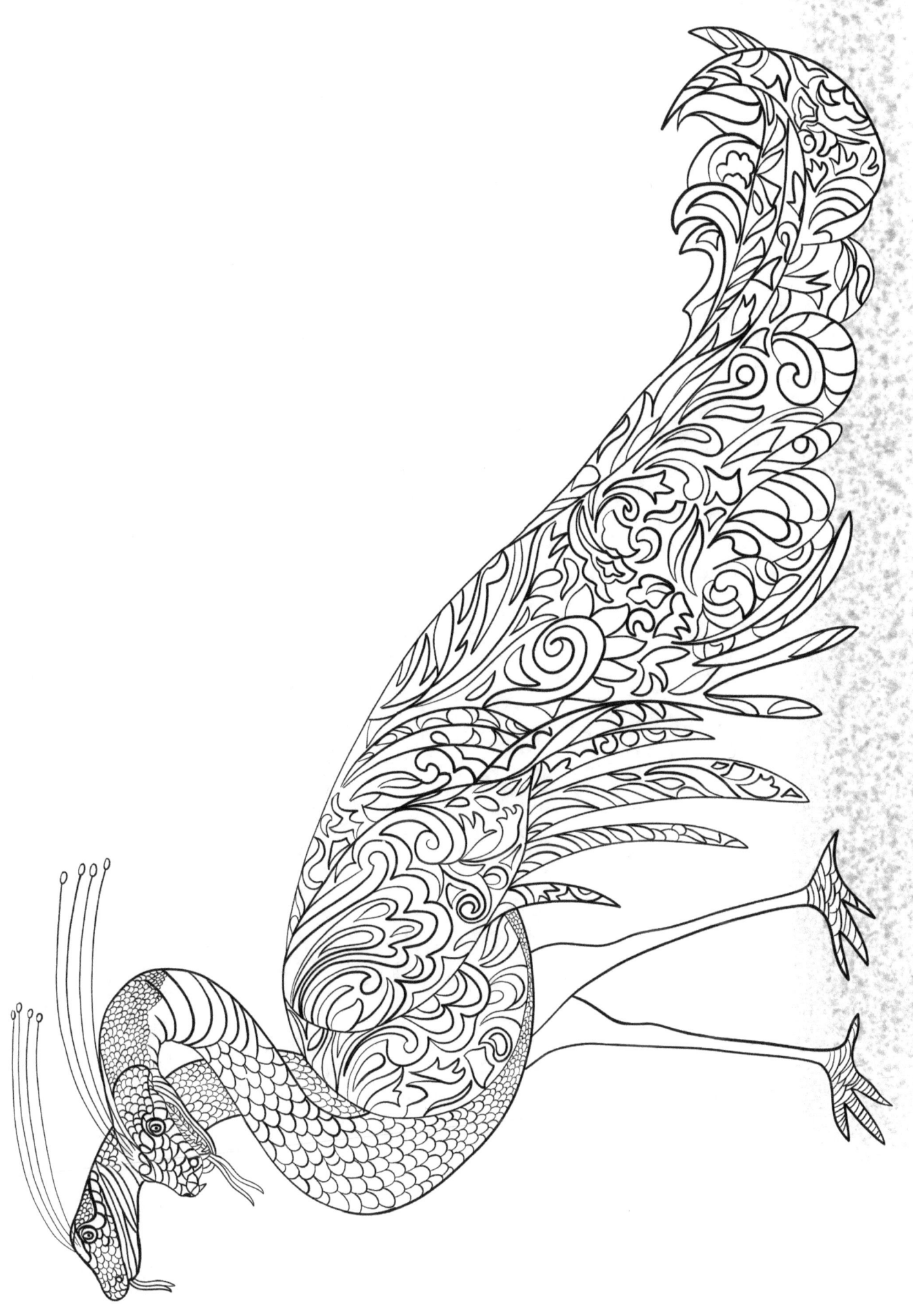

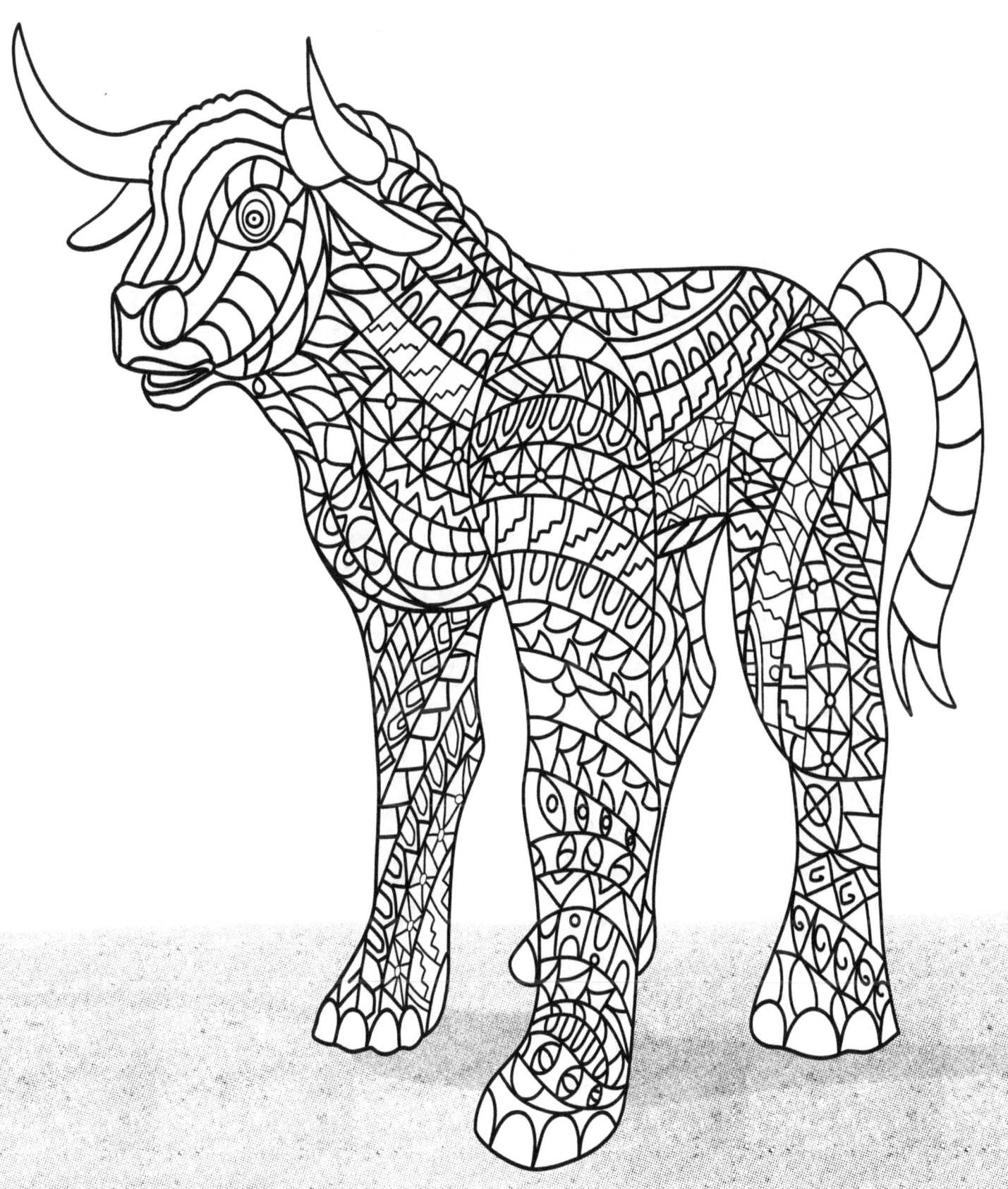

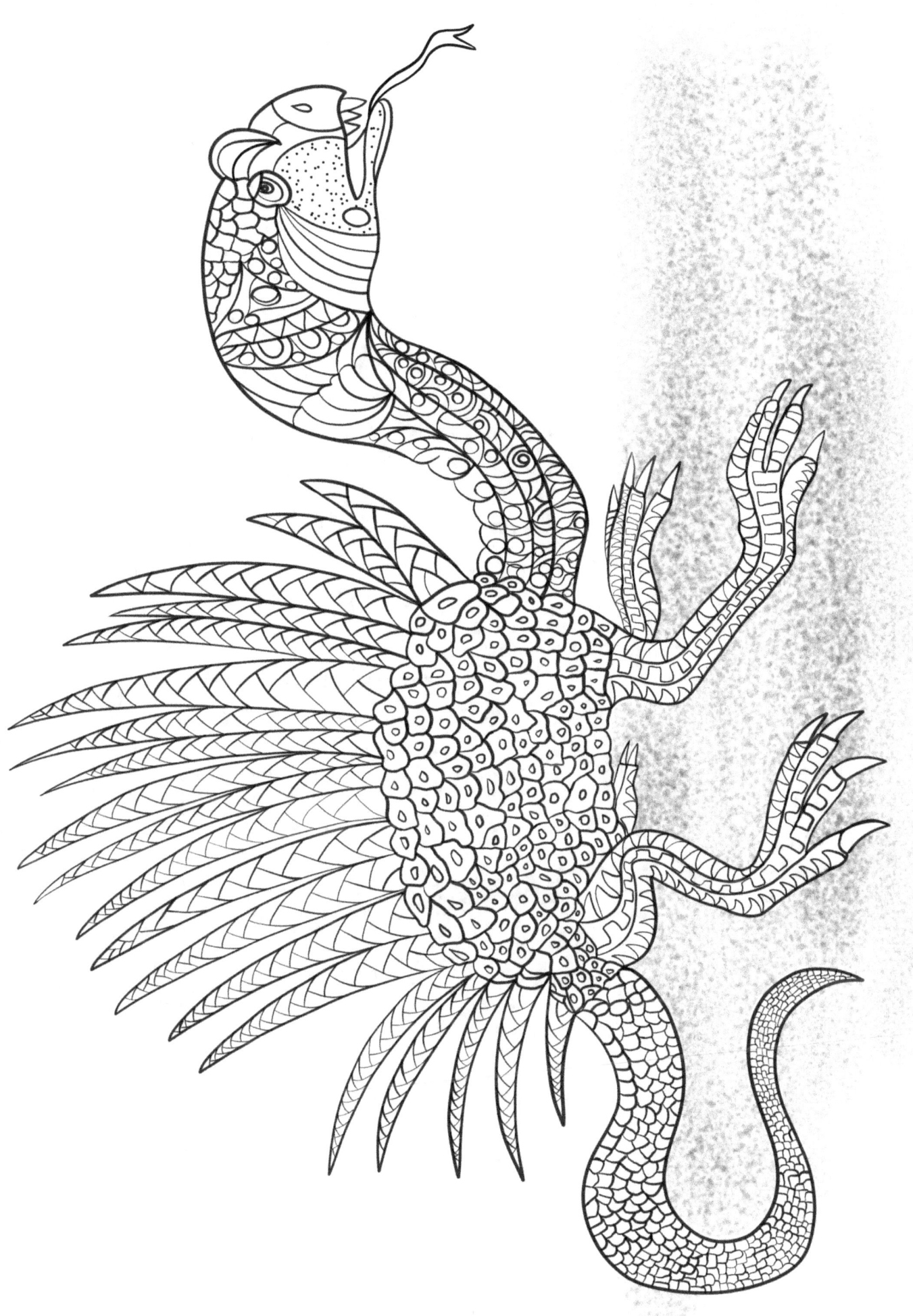

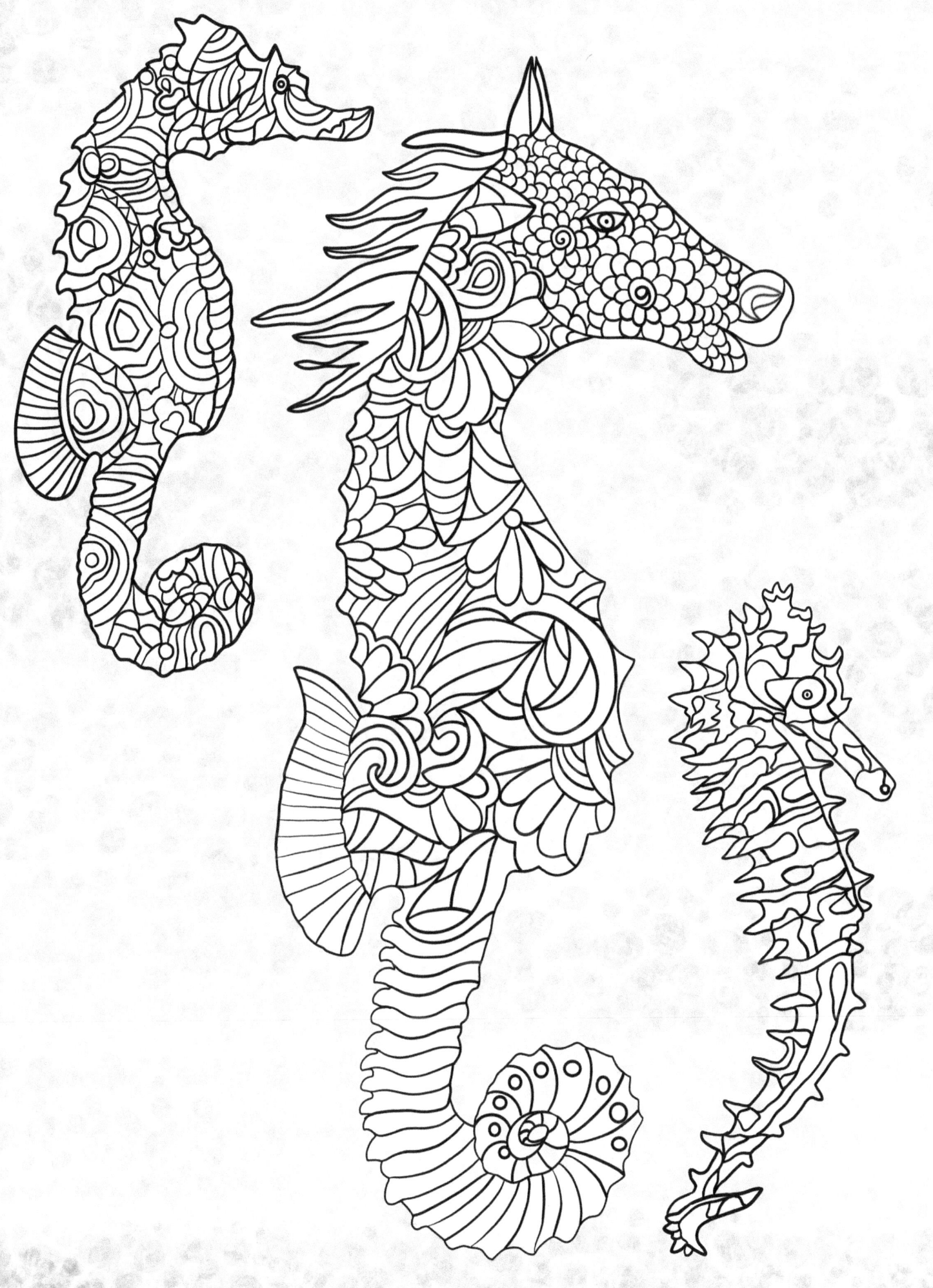

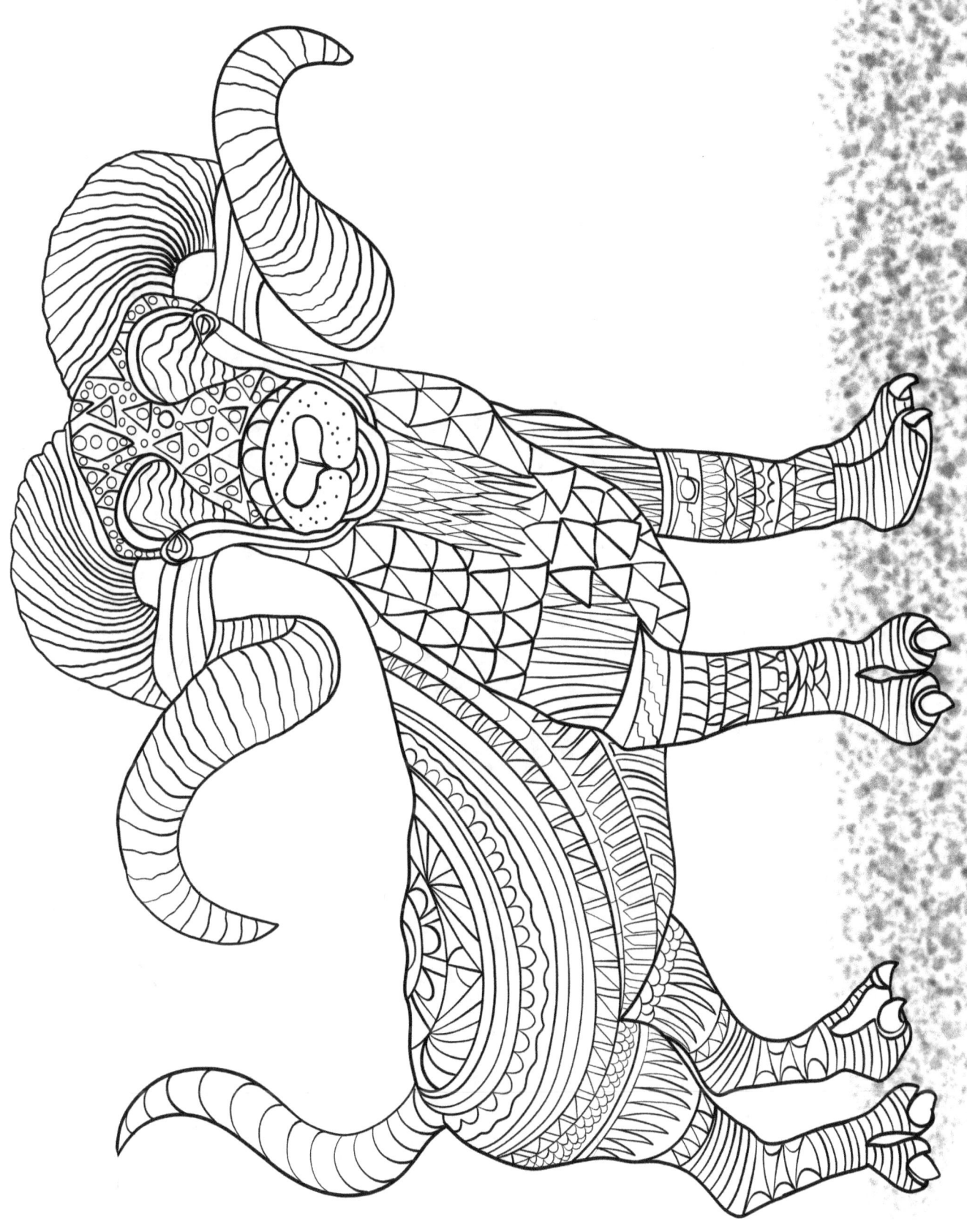

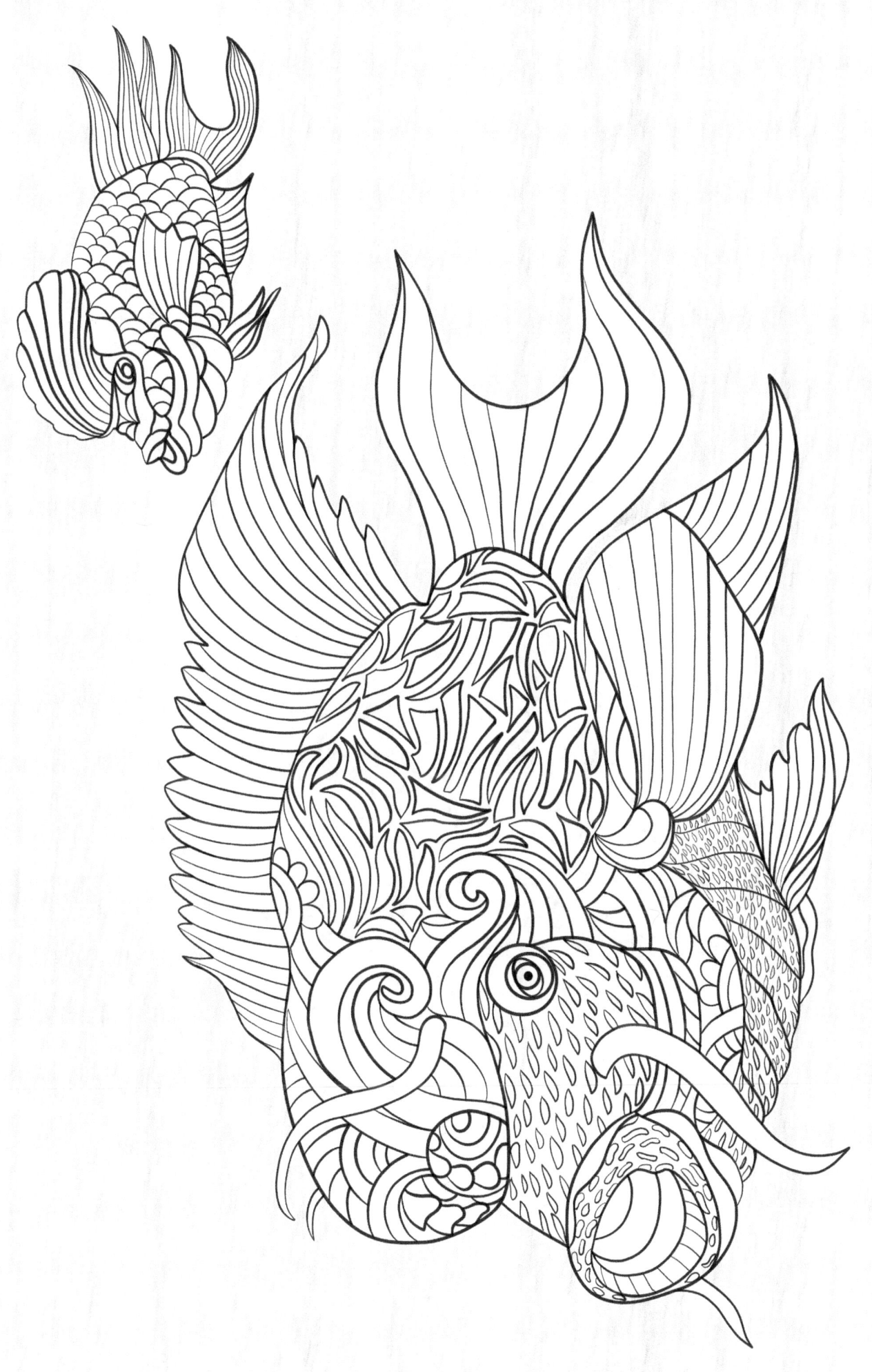

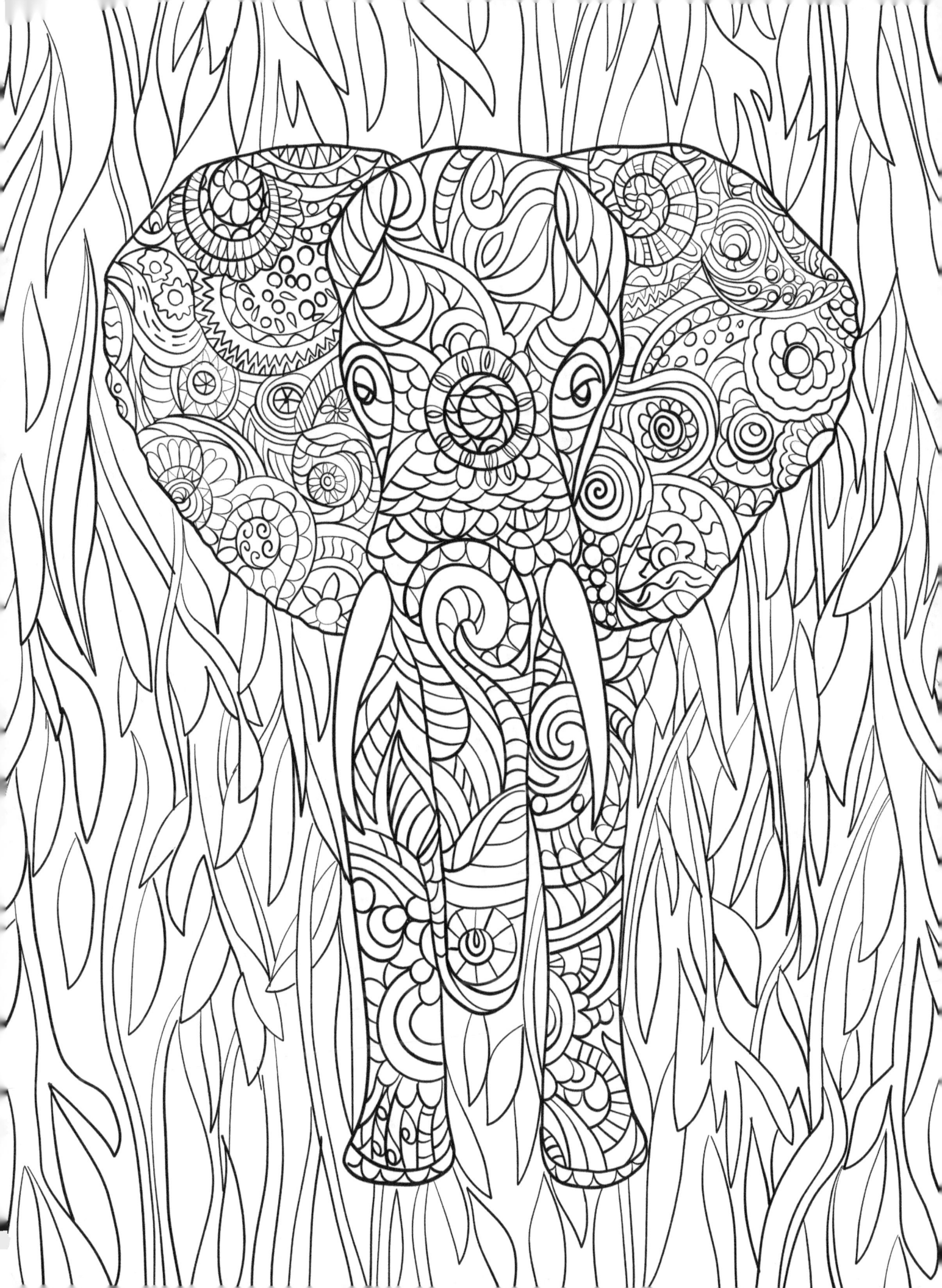

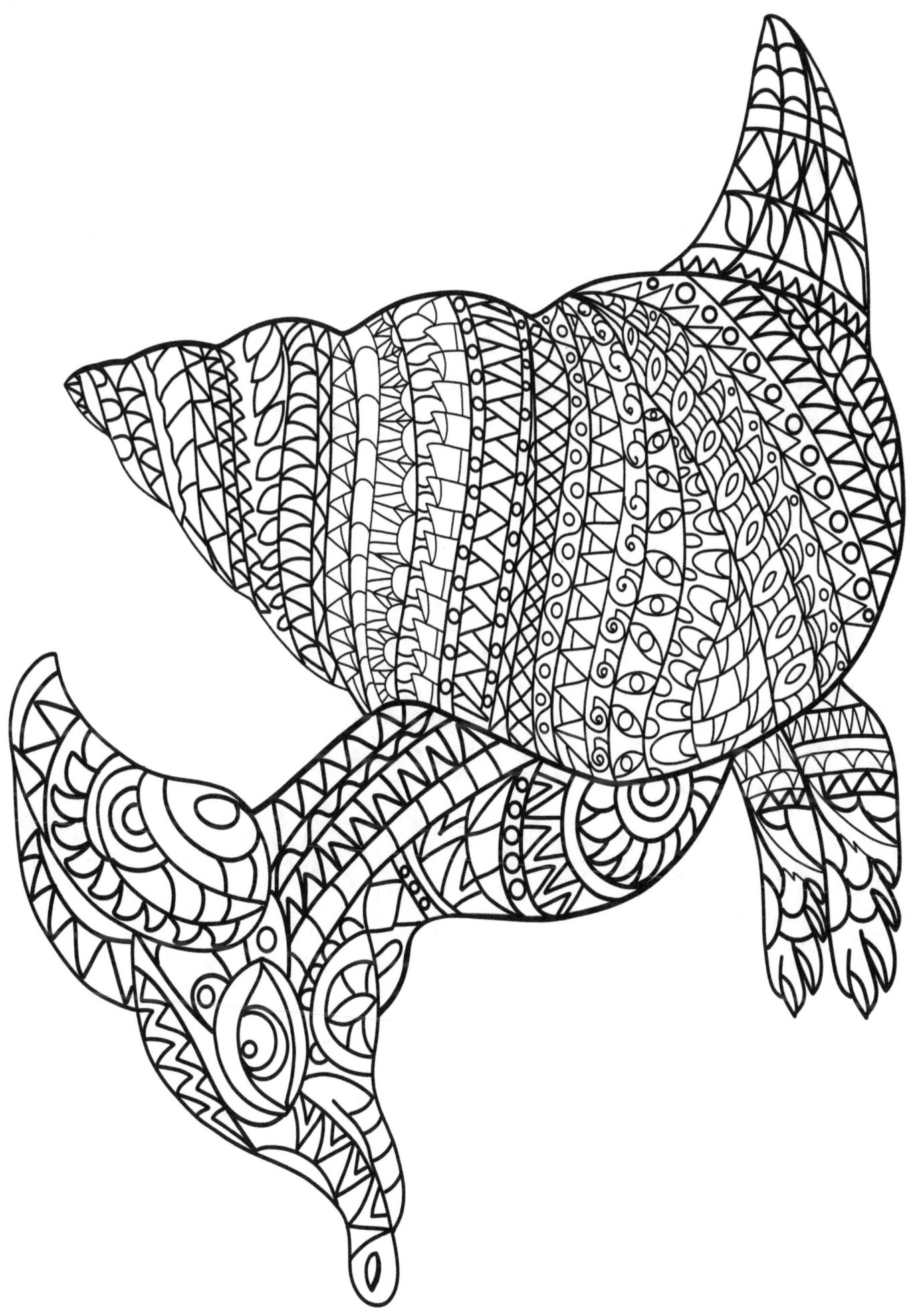

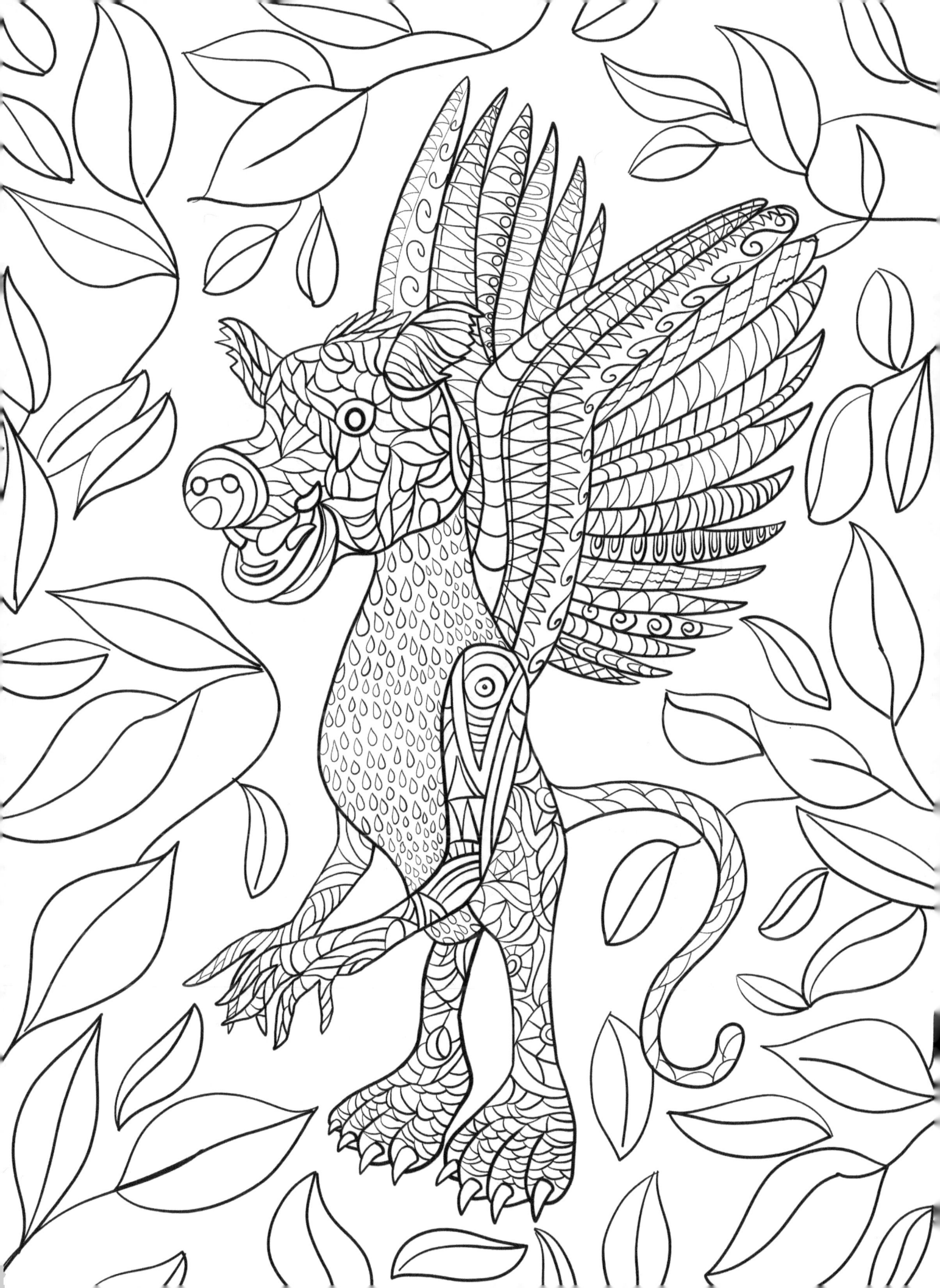

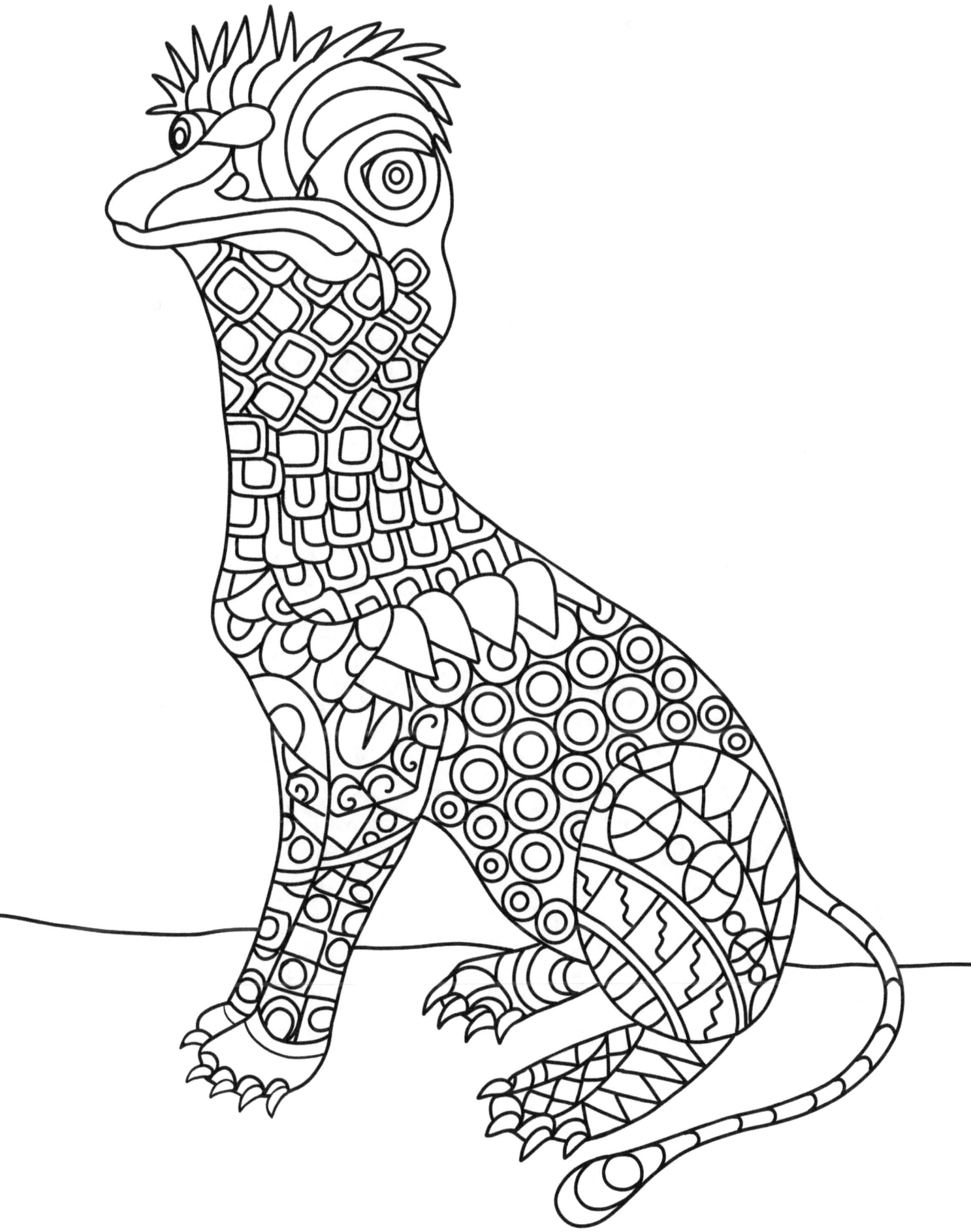

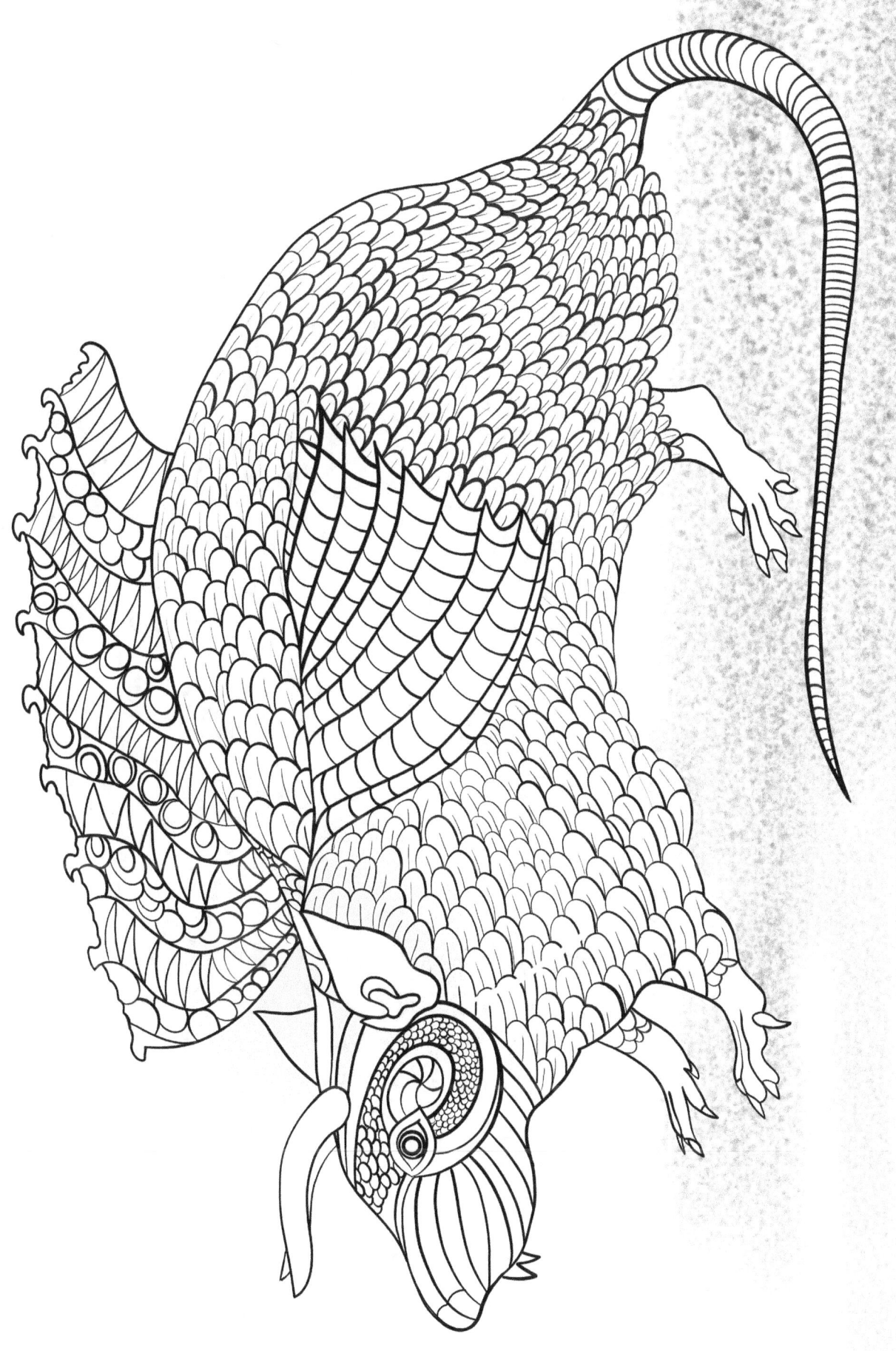

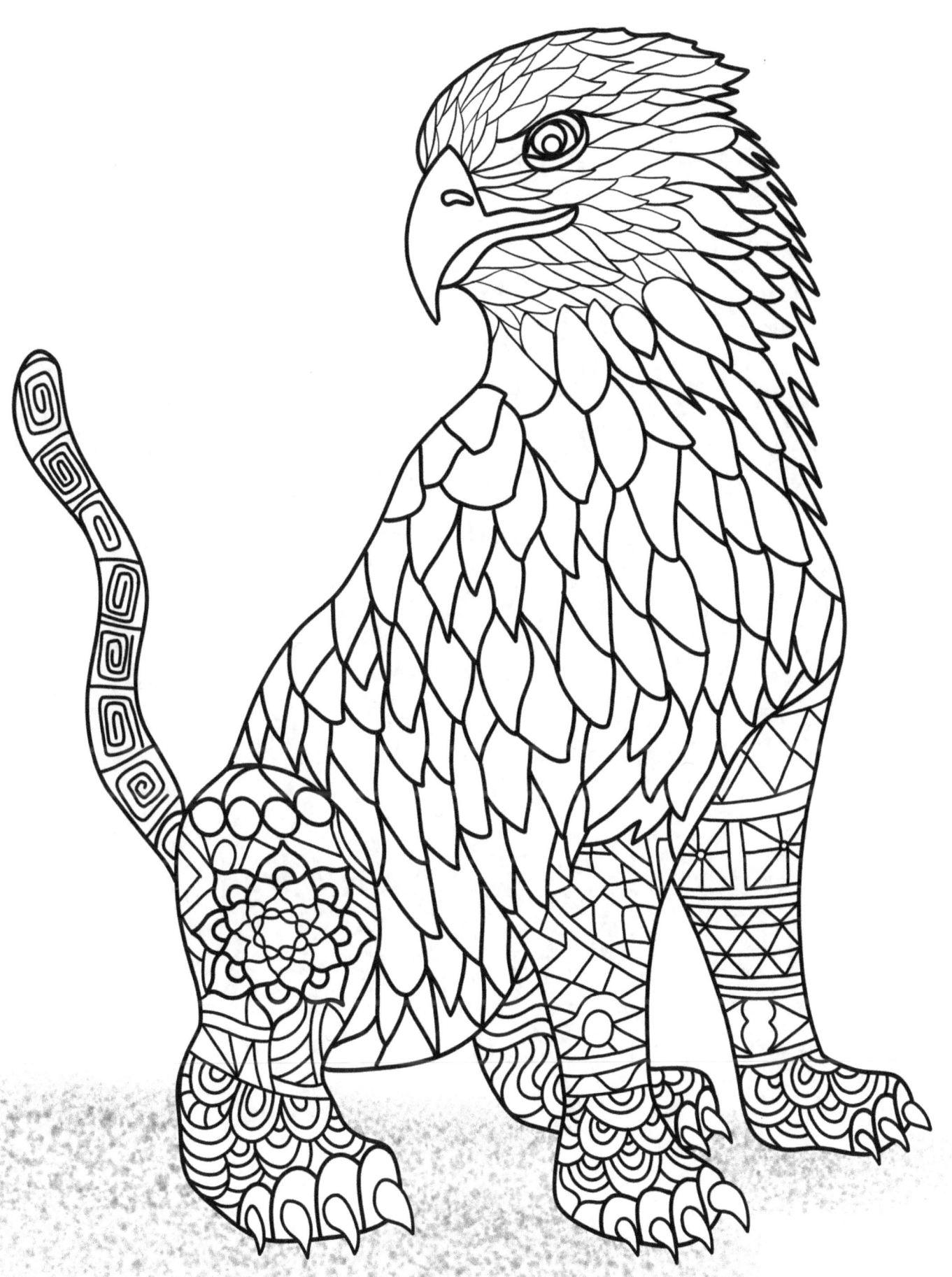

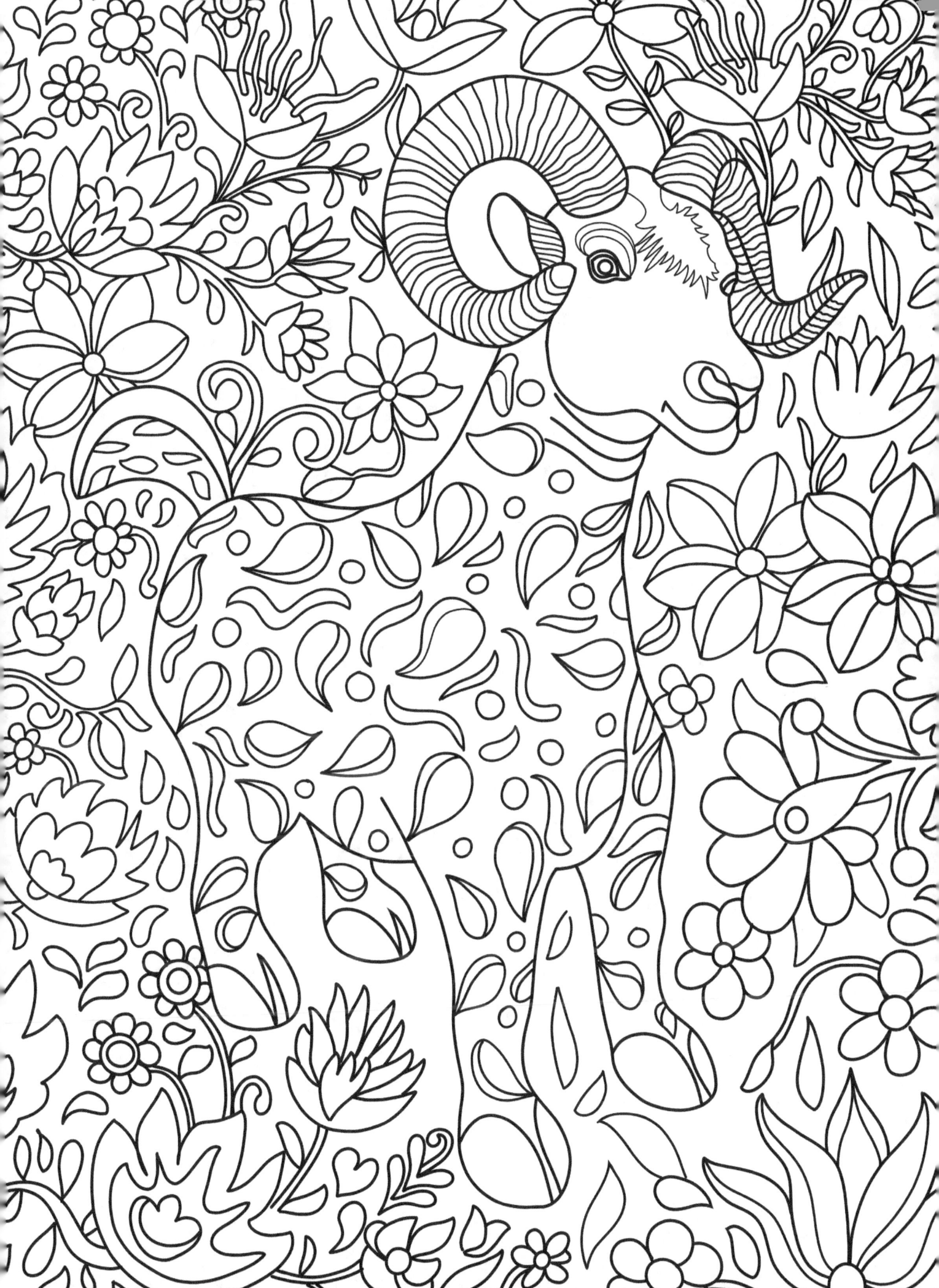

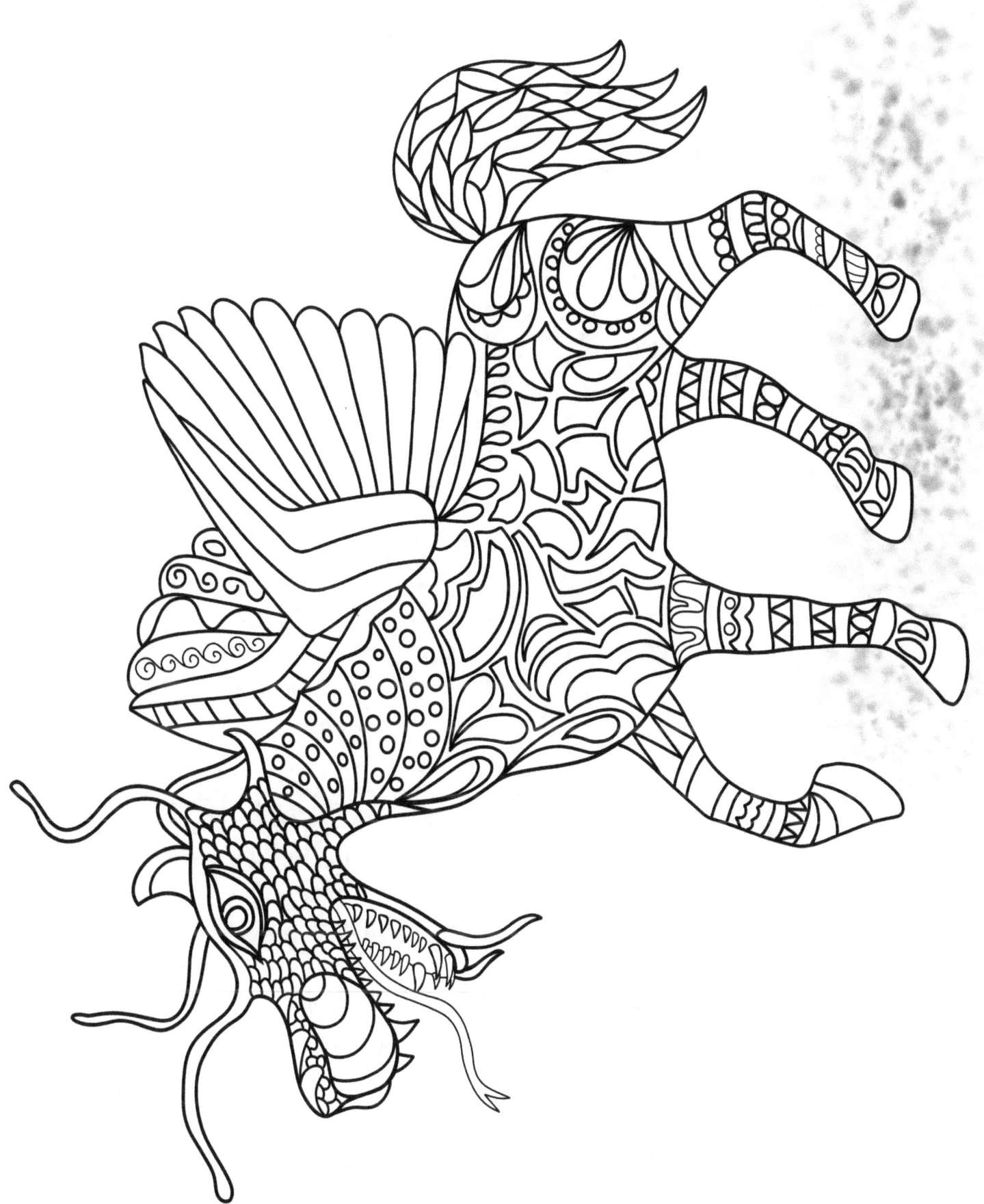

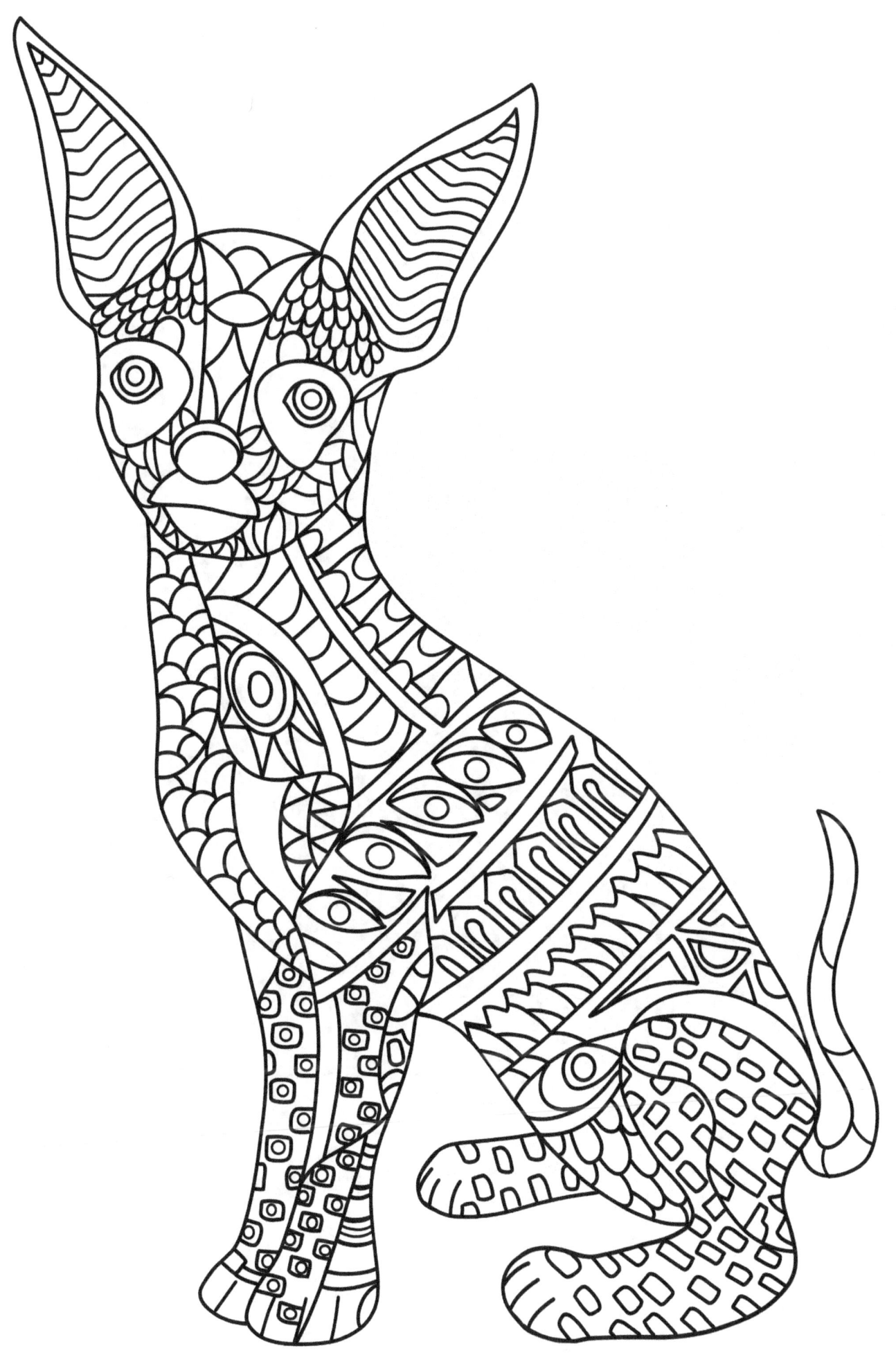

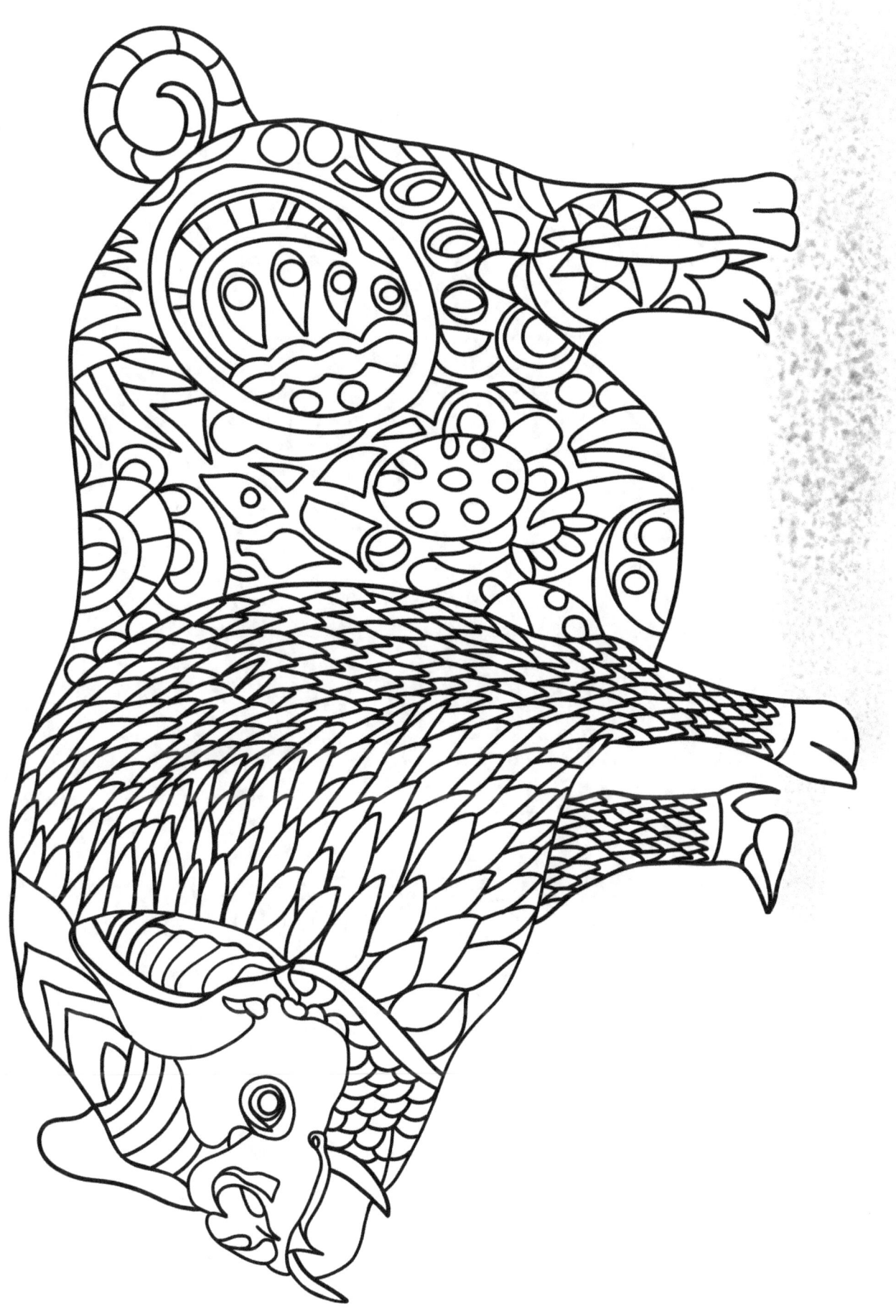

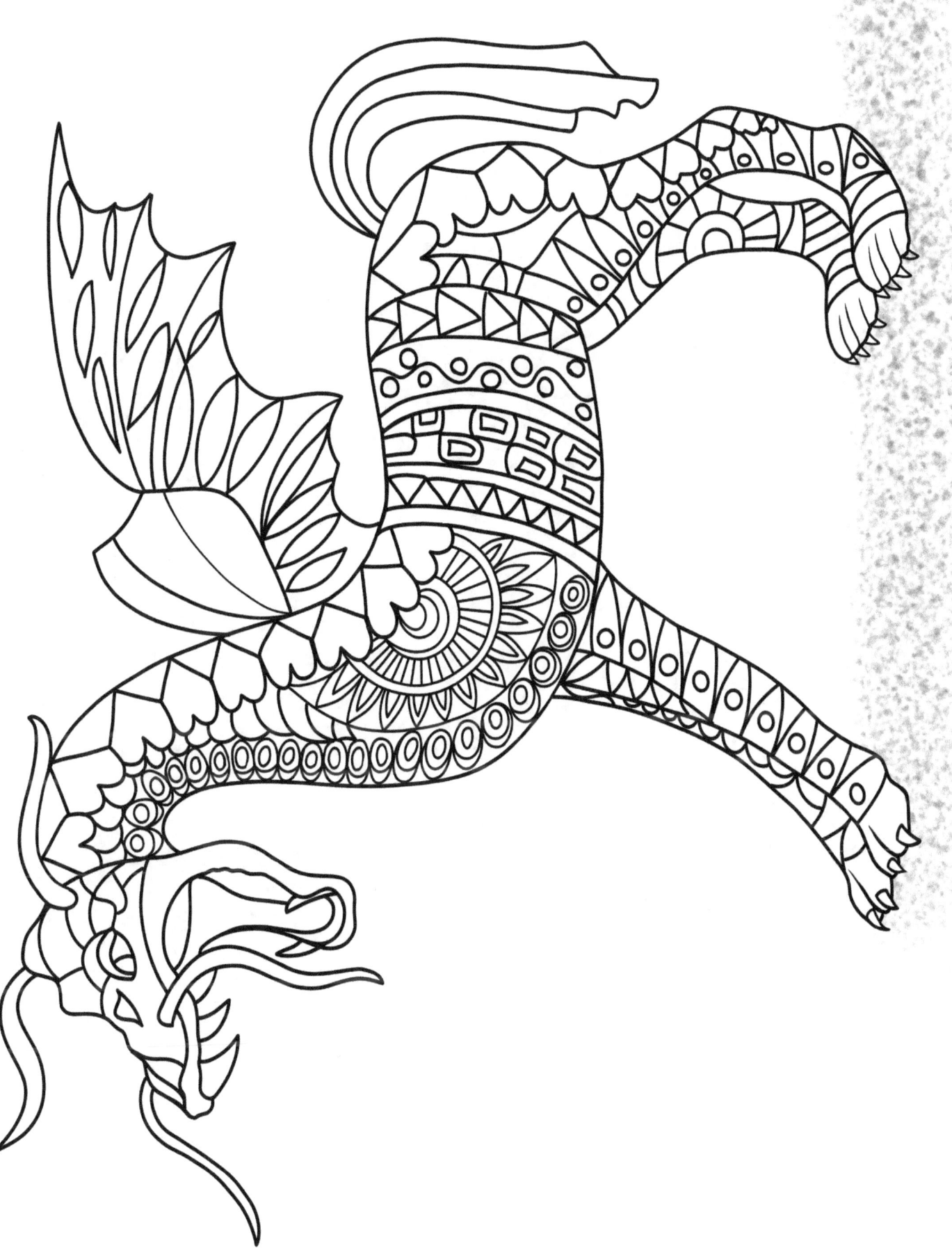

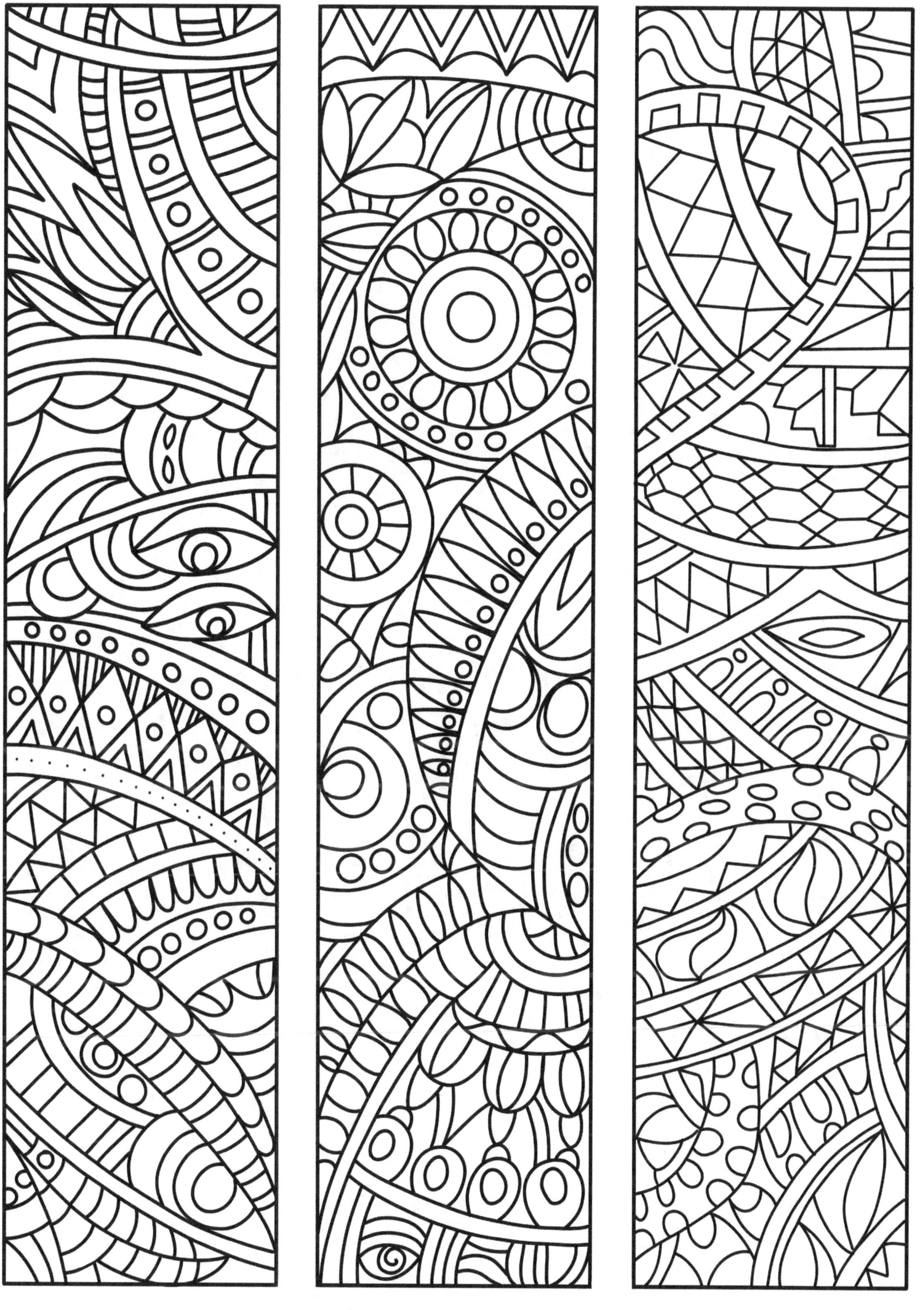

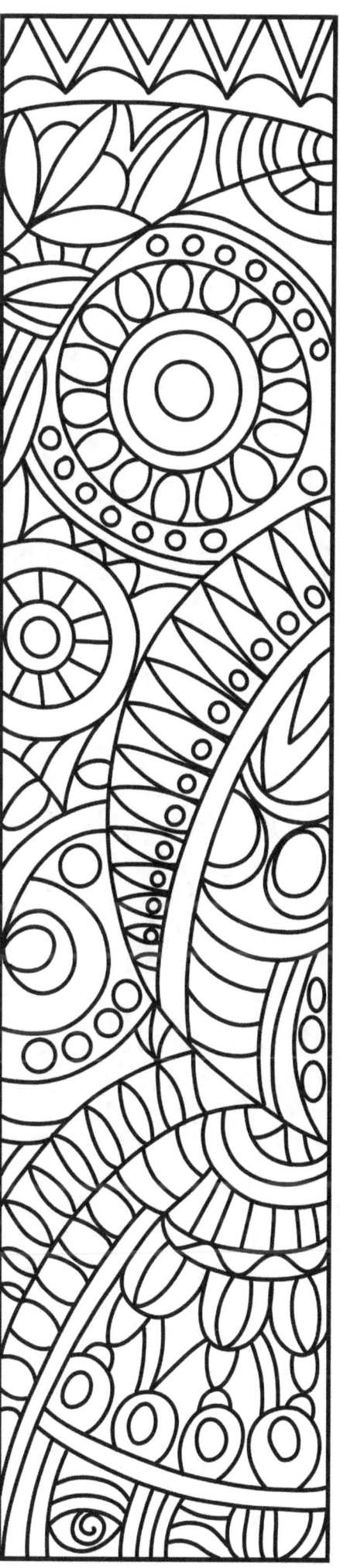
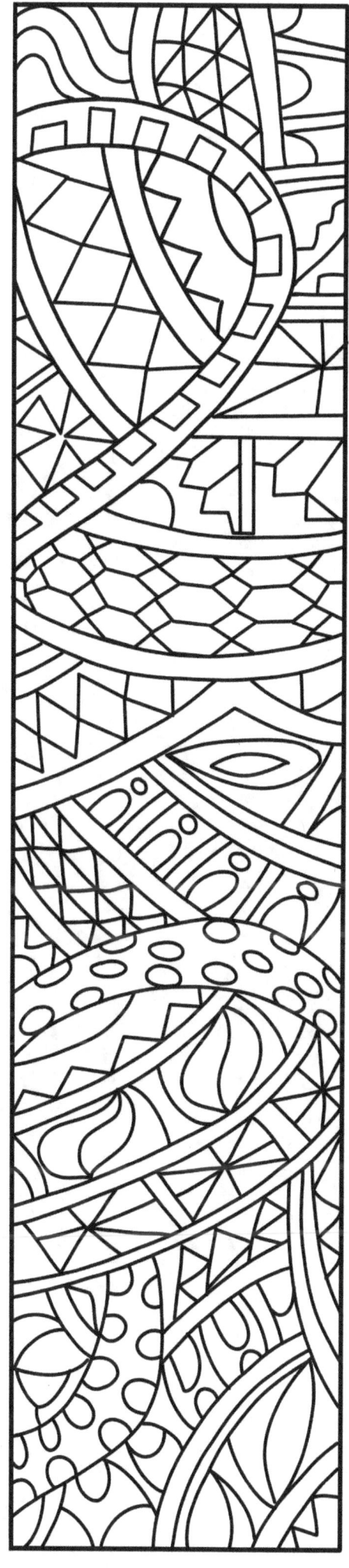

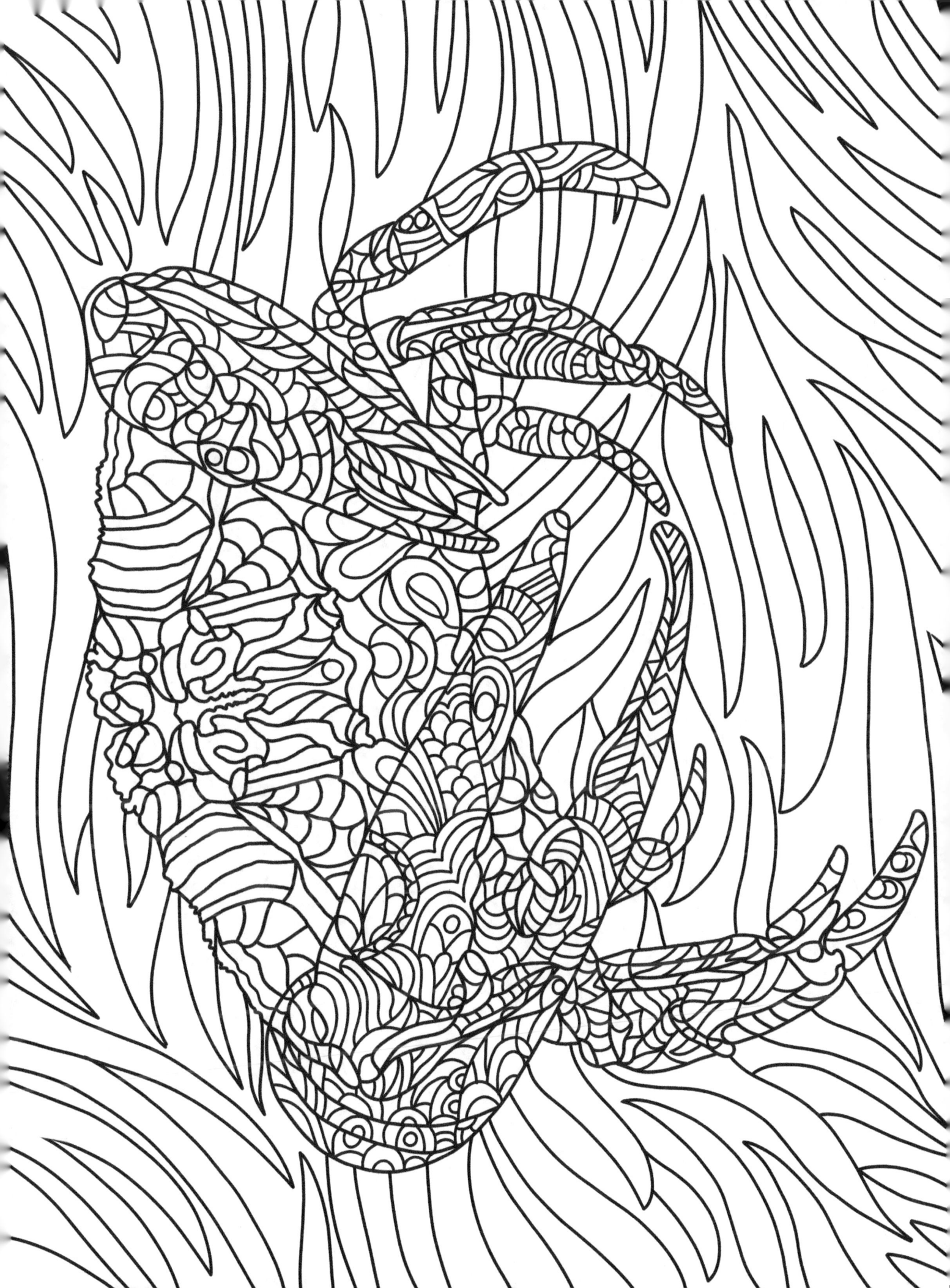

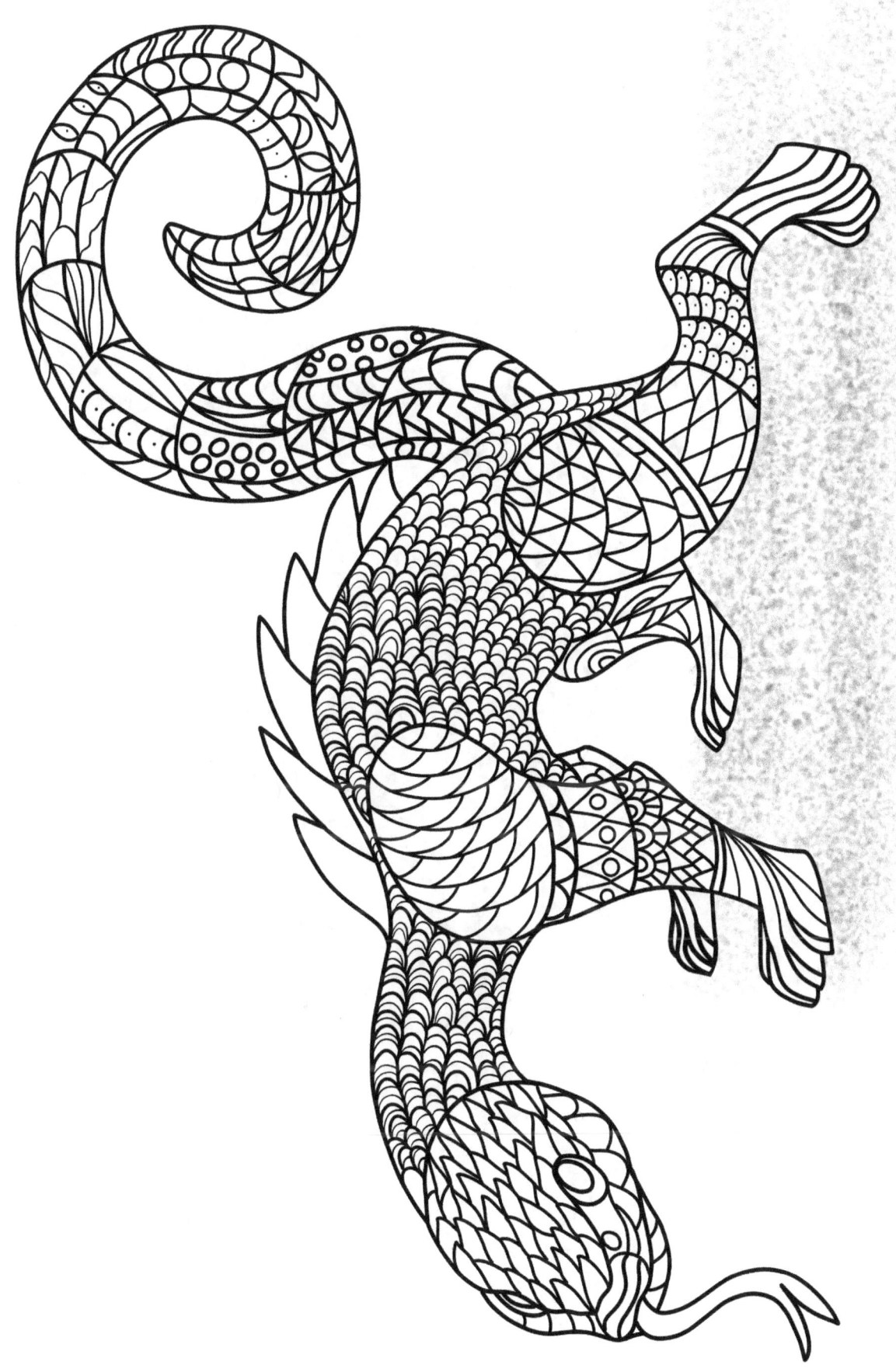

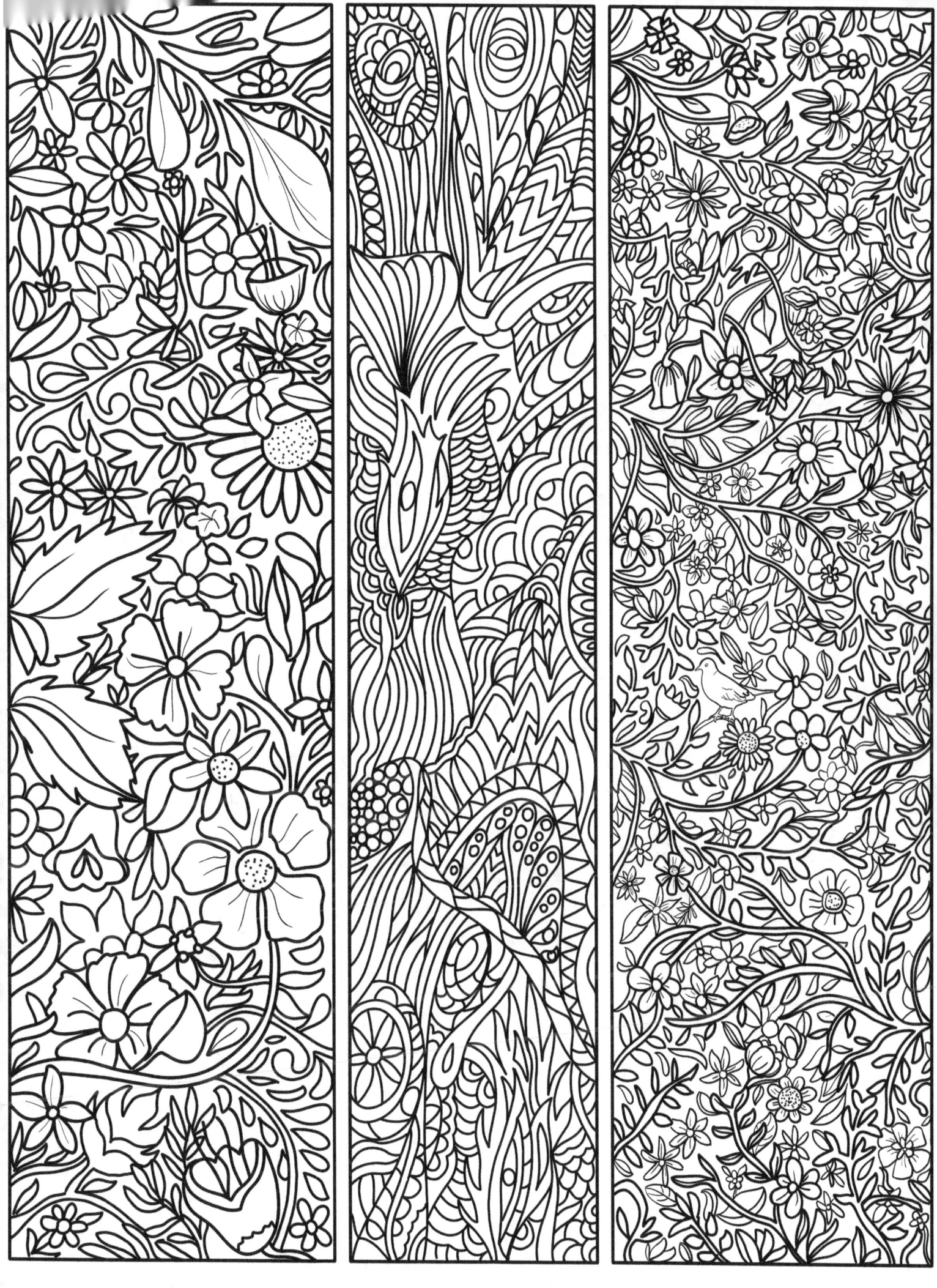

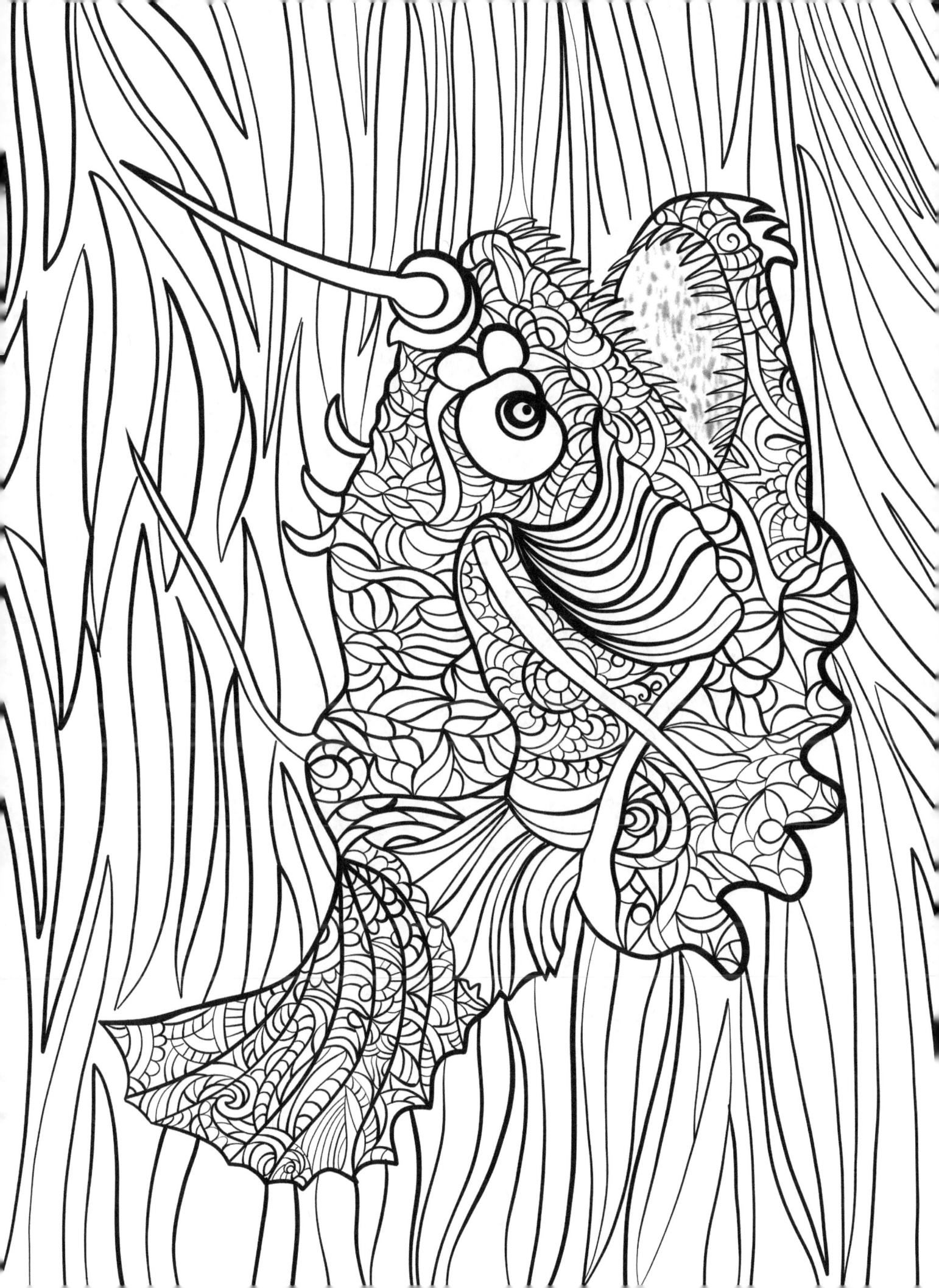

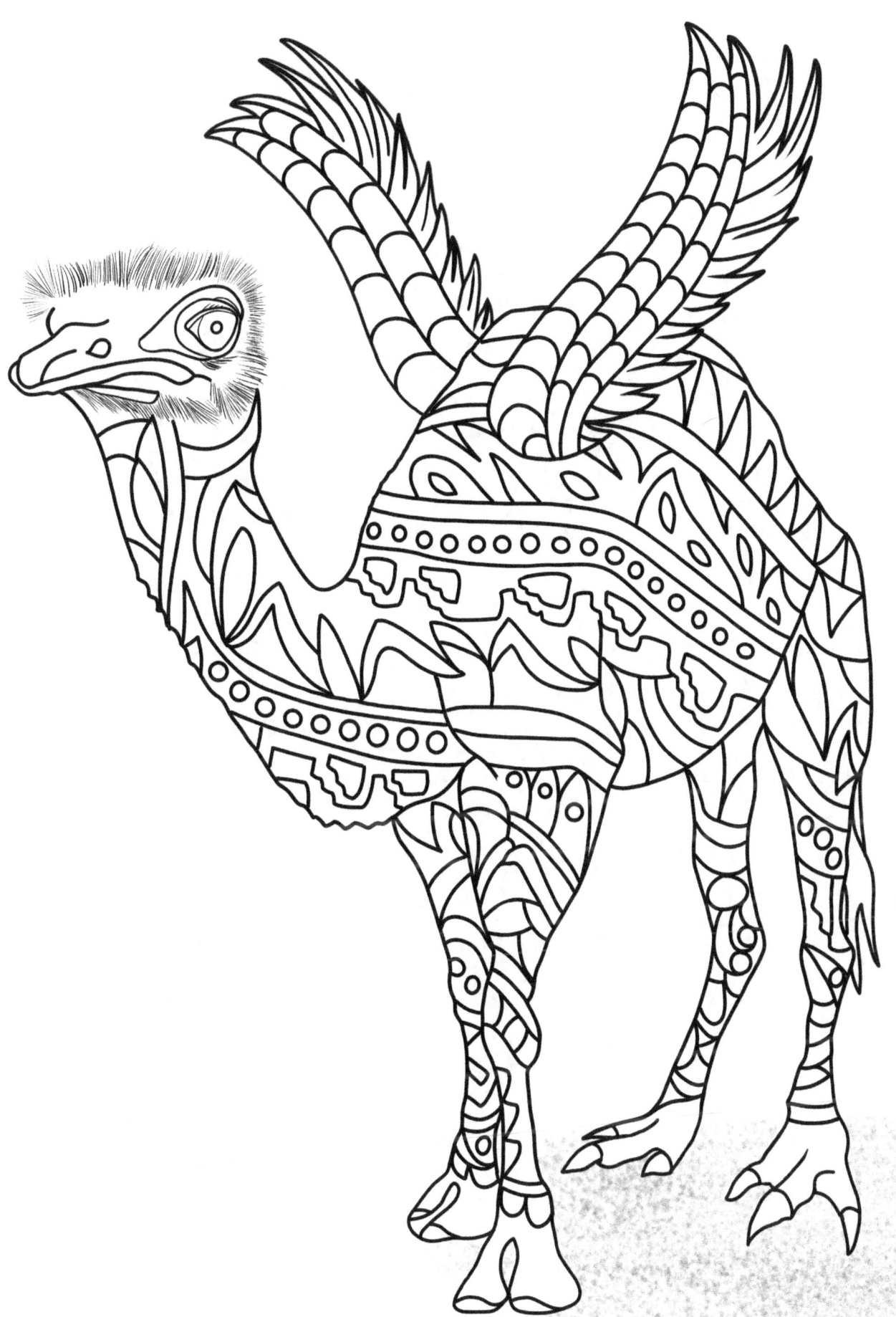

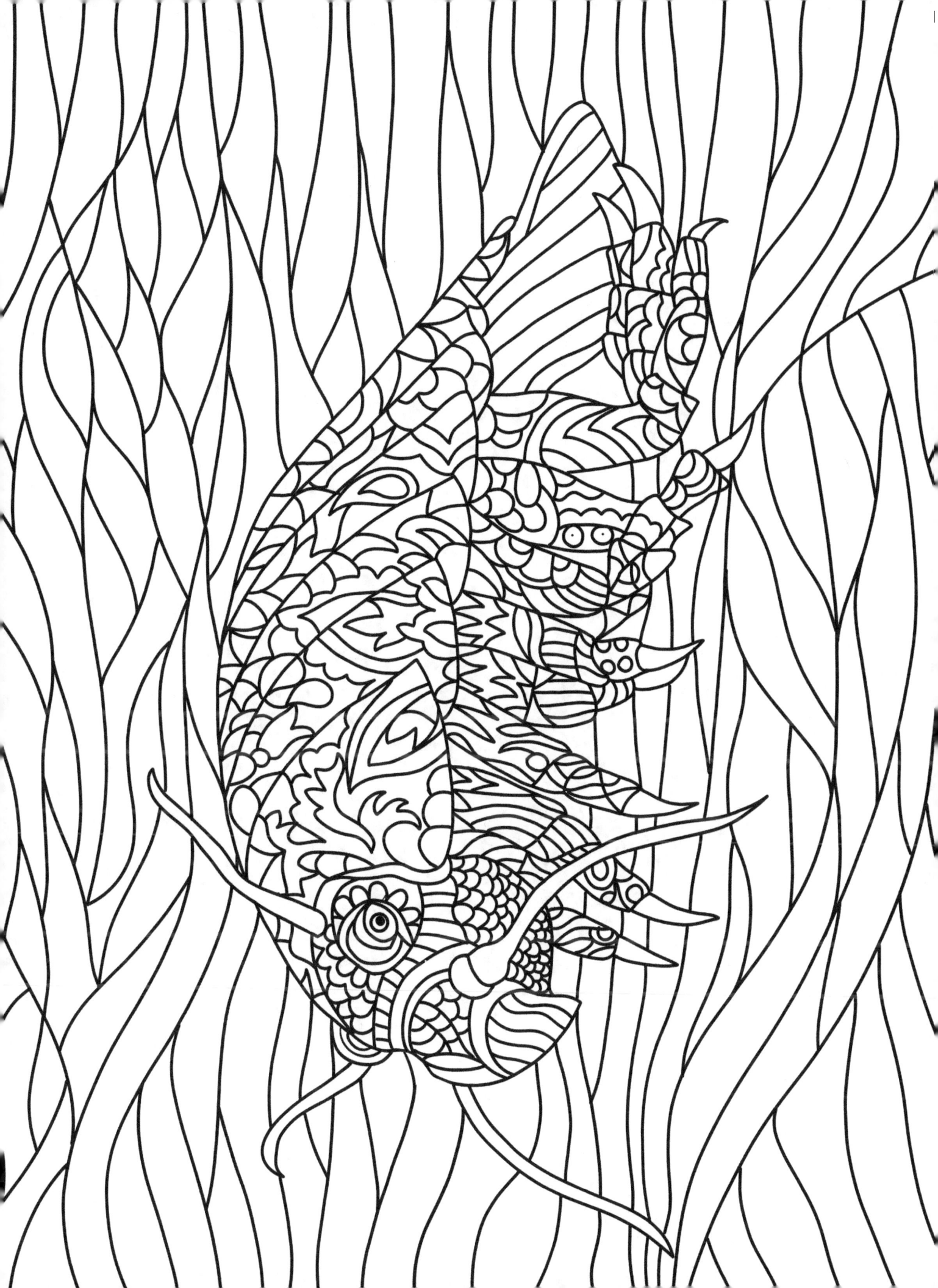

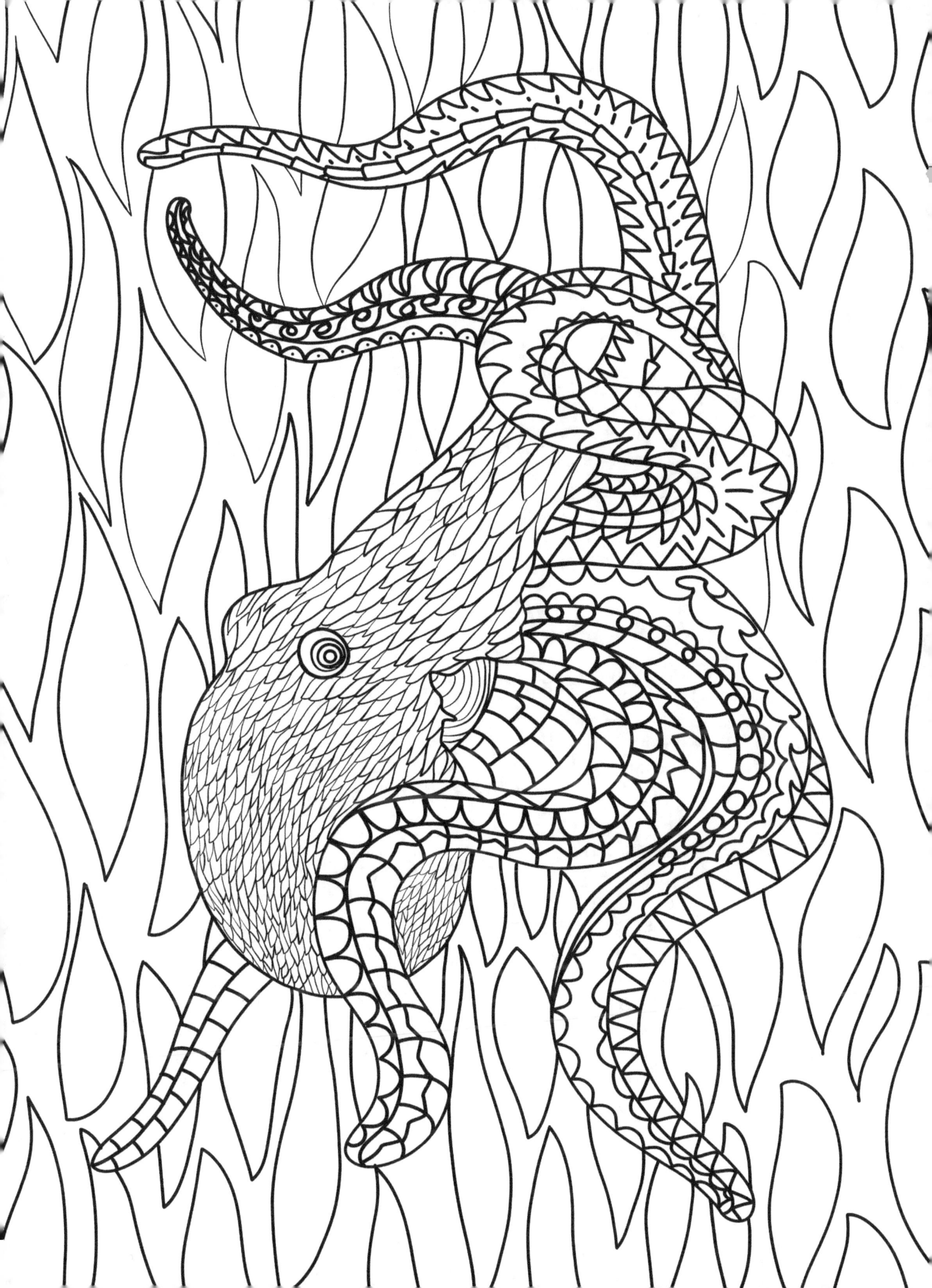

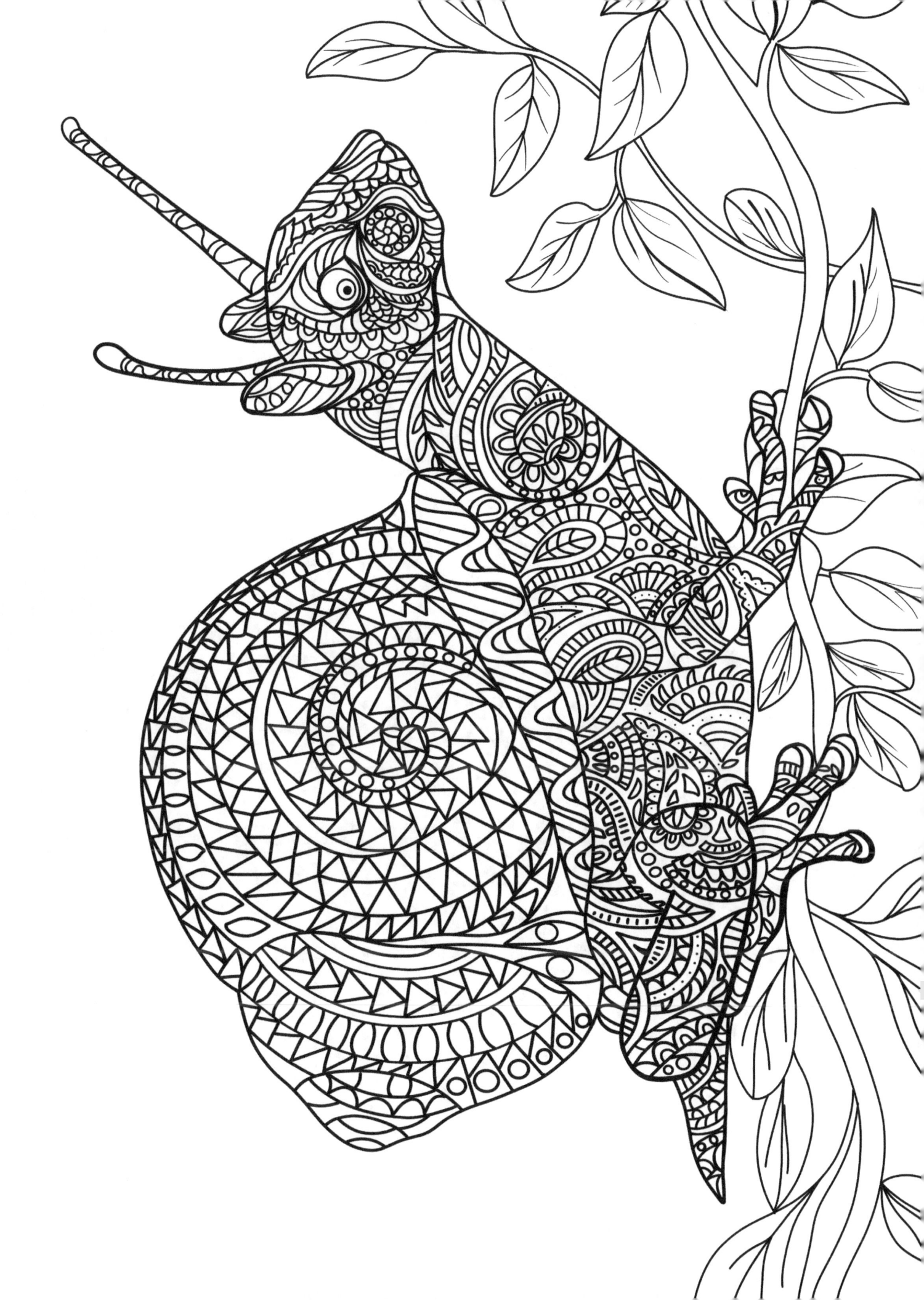

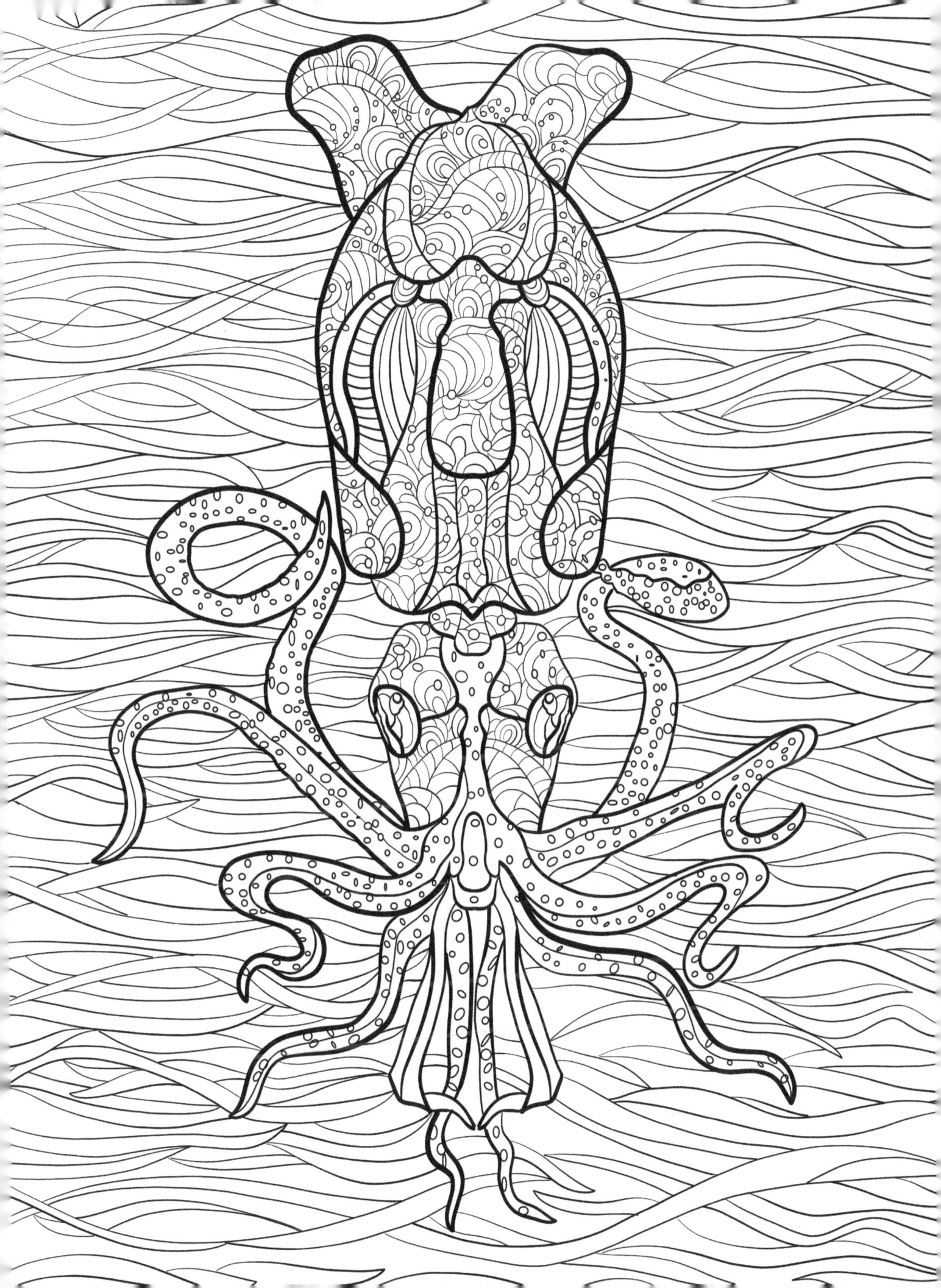

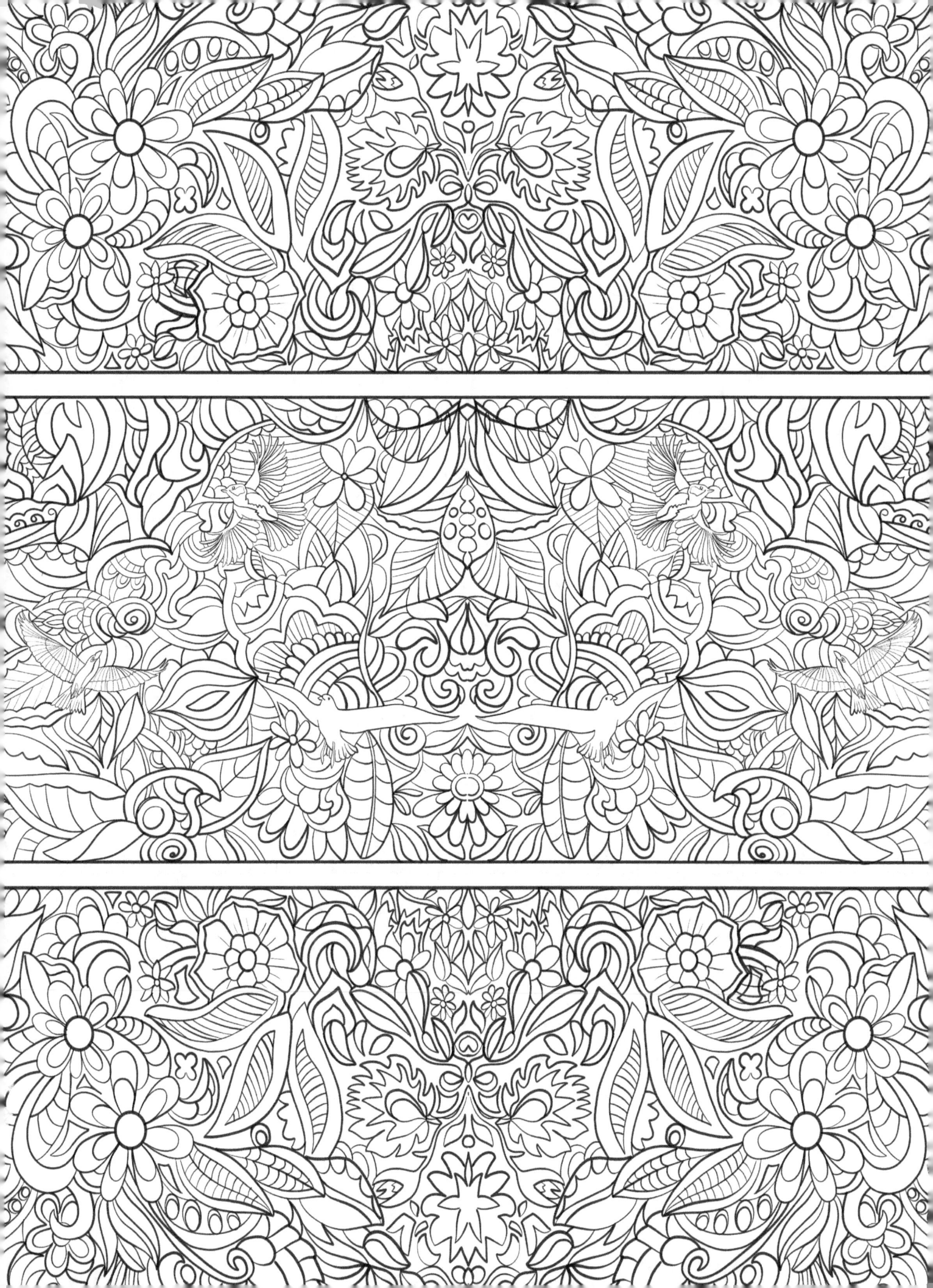

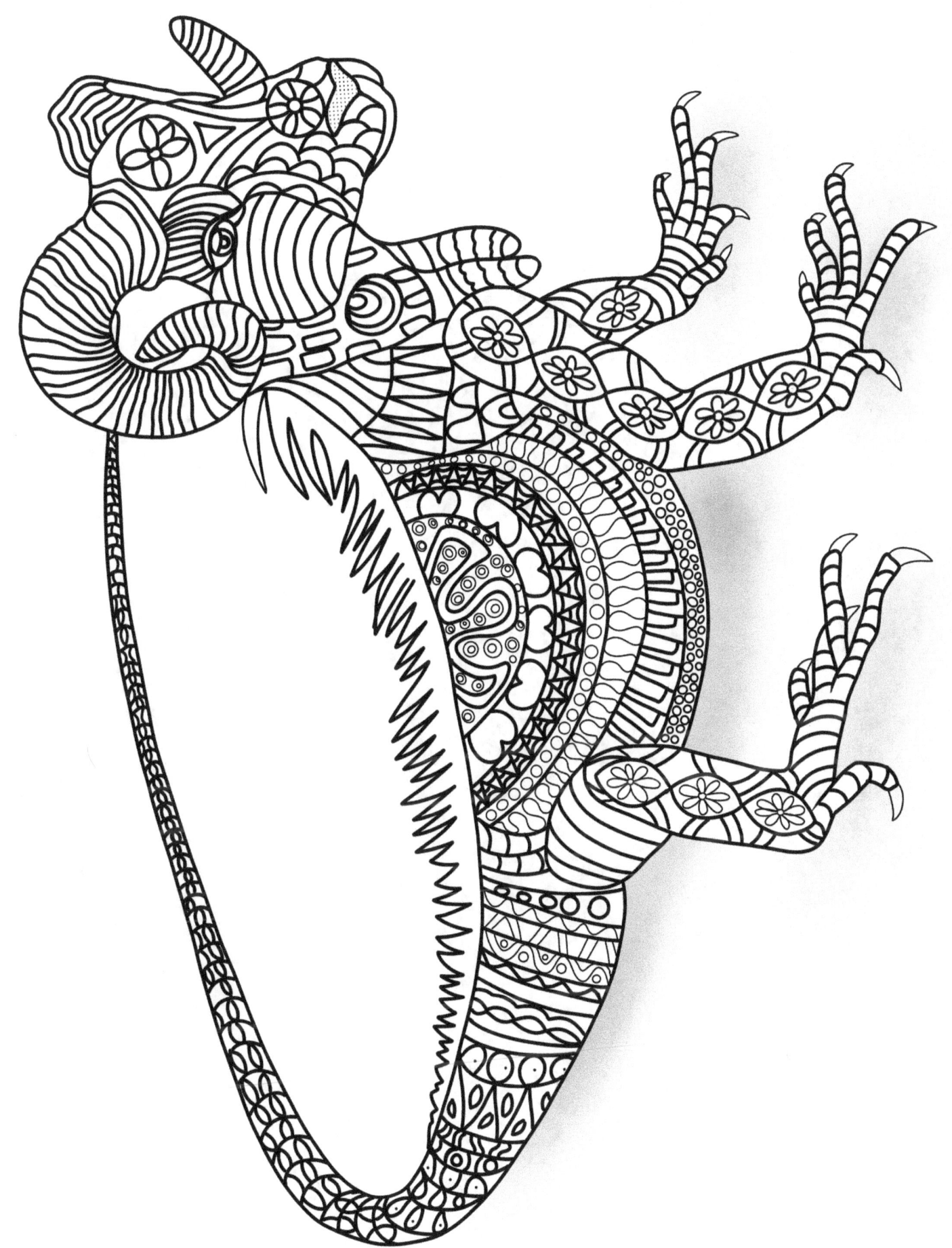

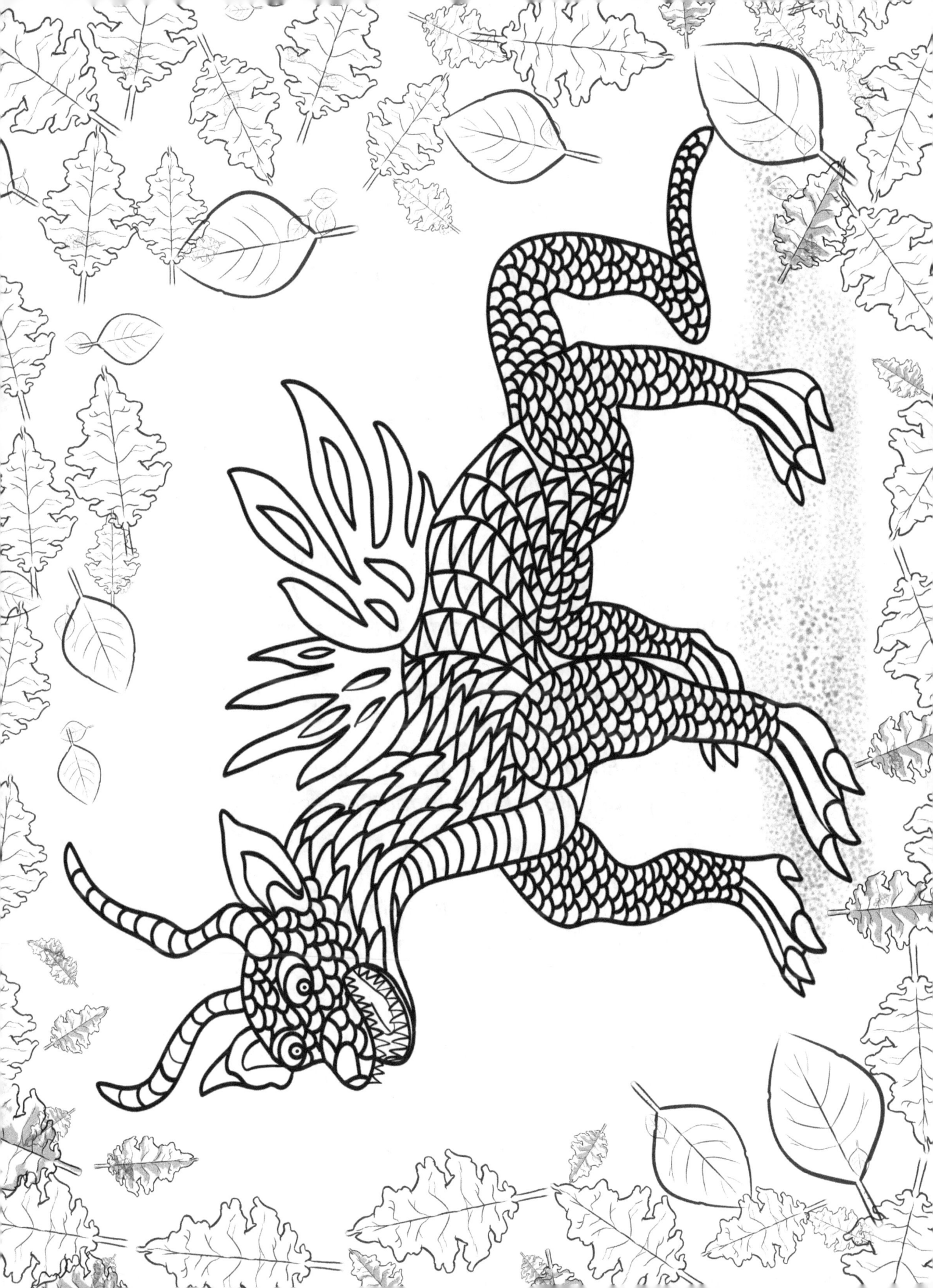

Also by Jorge Lulić

Colouring books

The Nymphs & Fairies
colouring book

Alebrijes series
Books 1 - 2 - 3 - 4

Ninfas y Hadas
libro de colorear
Available in English and Spanish

America Viva Pre-Columbian Art Colouring Book

Masks - Colouring Book - Inspired in Rapa Nui & Maori Art

Extinct & Endangered Animals Colouring Book
Available in English and Spanish

Mr Armadillo
Mr Armadillo colouring book
Available in English and Spanish

All books available from Amazon worldwide

www.jorgelulic.com

www.ingramcontent.com/pod-product-compliance
Lightning Source LLC
Chambersburg PA
CBHW082014230526
45468CB00022B/2225